A SPOONFUL OF *Sugar*

Sew 20 Simple Projects to Sweeten Your Surroundings Zakka Style

LISA COX

Fons&Porter
CINCINNATI, OHIO

CONTENTS

INTRODUCTION

Welcome to *A Spoonful of Sugar*. In this book you'll find twenty original, practical and sweet projects to decorate your home, bedroom, kitchen, craft room and playroom, or to give as one-of-a kind gifts. Most of the projects are suited for the confident beginner and intermediate sewist, and they can be made in an afternoon—perfect for the busy, time-poor crafter!

These sewing projects incorporate a number of techniques for embellishment, including patchwork, raw-edge appliqué, crochet, chicken scratch embroidery and sashiko. By customizing your handmade creations, you will be able to put your own unique and modern twist on your project.

I have always loved the process of creating. My favorite pastime as a child was anything that involved crafts. I was happiest when I had fabric, yarn and thread to create with. I was born into a family that valued handmade items, and I grew up watching my mum and grandmother sew, crochet, knit, embroider, create floral arrangements and decorate cakes.

Although I didn't have the opportunity to study home economics at school, my mother taught me the basics of sewing and was always happy to let me use her Singer sewing machine on the kitchen table. I started by making doll clothes, then progressed to sewing my own clothing when I was a university student. My interest in crafts was rekindled when I had my own home and family, and I began making home décor items, kids' clothing and toys. Then, while we lived in Texas for a few years, I got hooked on quilting.

In 2008, together with my daughter Sarah (who was eleven years old at the time), I started a craft and baking blog, *A Spoonful of Sugar*, to document our creative pursuits. We have shared many sewing tutorials, craft projects and recipes over the years. We have really enjoyed being part of the blogging community, and our craft and sewing skills have evolved over time. We have made many friends, and it's wonderful to be able to share our creative passions with like-minded people.

Life can be hectic at times, so there is something therapeutic about sewing and crafts. It's a treat to take some time out of your busy day to choose fabrics and supplies and then to work on a project that allows you to express your creativity. Adding some embroidery or crochet provides the opportunity to take some time to enjoy the process of handwork. It's fun to see your project develop and to gain satisfaction from making something yourself. As an occupational therapist, I see the value in engaging in meaningful activity to promote a positive effect on health and well-being. Sewing can be a way to manage your stress and to improve your confidence and self-esteem. Nothing beats the joy of giving someone a beautiful gift that you made yourself!

I hope the projects in this book will inspire you to get creative and to learn some new techniques for embellishing your projects. If you're new to sewing, start with one of the easier projects, such as the *Ladybug Beanbag Game* or the *Crisscross Coasters*. Most of all, have fun and happy sewing!

Lisa Cox
www.aspoonfulofsugardesigns.com

TOOLS AND MATERIALS

Sewing, like any hobby, has a wide range of tools and gadgets available. Here's an overview of the essential tools and materials required for creating the projects in this book, as well as recommendations for some nonessential tools that can be added to improve results and make craft time more enjoyable. Good-quality tools give the best results and generally last longer. You can find most of these tools at your local craft or quilt store.

BASIC SEWING TOOLS

Sewing machine
Universal sewing machine needle
Cotton sewing thread
Iron and ironing board
Pressing cloth
Seam ripper
Measuring tape
Pins and pincushion
Fabric shears
Hand-sewing needles
Rotary cutter and self-healing mat
Acrylic gridded ruler
Water-soluble fabric pen

SEWING MACHINES AND ACCESSORIES

Sewing Machine

An extensive range of sewing machines are on the market, from very simple, entry-level sewing machines to complex computerized machines that have more features and stitches. To construct the projects in this book, you will need a sewing machine with the following basic functions:

✳ adjustable stitch length and width

✳ zigzag stitch

You will need a standard presser foot, a zipper foot and a ¼" (6mm) foot. A walking foot is helpful if your machine does not have a built-in dual feed.

When choosing a new sewing machine, look for one that has features you will use. Shop around and be sure to test drive the machines in the store to find one that will be a good fit for your needs.

Sewing Machine Needles

Sewing machine needles come in a variety of sizes, and it's important to use the appropriate needle for the project you're working on. Most of the projects in this book can be made with a universal needle (size 80/12), which is suited to most woven cotton fabrics. A denim needle (size 100/16) is recommended when sewing jeans or other projects that use denim. Check your sewing machine manual for more information on needles suited to your machine.

Needles get dull over time and can break, so you'll need to change them regularly to ensure your stitching is even. It's a good idea to change the needle after every project or two.

Serger (Overlocker)

A serger is a type of sewing machine that cuts the edges of the seam allowance as they are fed through the machine, then overlocks the raw edge to give a neat and professional finish to the seam allowance. A serger is an optional machine in the construction of the projects in this book. If you make a lot of clothing and home décor items, it can be a good investment.

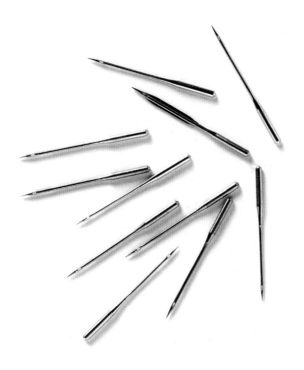

TIP

Clean your machine often to remove lint and fibers. Review your sewing machine manual for other important maintenance checks.

CUTTING TOOLS

Scissors

Most crafters will require several pairs of scissors to use for different purposes. You will need the following:

* **Fabric shears:** Shears usually have an 8"–10" (20.3cm–25.4cm) blade and are used for cutting fabric. Be sure to label them "fabric only" to avoid someone accidentally using them to cut paper. Cutting paper or other materials will dull the blade. Sharpen your fabric shears occasionally to keep the blades sharp and working smoothly.

* **Pinking shears:** Pinking shears are great for minimizing fraying on raw edges and creating decorative edges on ribbon and felt.

* **Embroidery scissors:** These are small scissors with thin, sharp blades. They are perfect for cutting threads and intricate appliqué shapes.

* **Craft scissors:** These are standard scissors for cutting paper, card and other craft supplies.

Rotary Cutter and Self-Healing Mat

Rotary cutters have sharp, retractable blades and are able to cut through several layers of fabric simultaneously. Rotary cutters are available in a range of sizes. A 45mm blade is a versatile size for small projects. Always have a replacement blade on hand for when the blade becomes dull.

Protect your table surface and blade from damage by using a self-healing cutting mat. An 18" × 24" (45.7cm × 61cm) mat is a good size for small projects. Cutting mats have a 1" (2.5cm) grid, which is useful for cutting and measuring your fabric.

MEASURING AND MARKING TOOLS

Acrylic Gridded Rulers
Clear gridded rulers are designed for use with your rotary cutter to assist in accurately cutting fabric for patchwork and other sewing projects. It is recommended to have a few different sizes on hand to suit the projects you work on frequently. Useful sizes include 6" × 12" (15.2cm × 30.4cm), 5" × 24" (12.7cm × 61cm) and 4" × 4" (10.2cm × 10.2cm).

Tape Measure
Made of flexible plastic, a dressmaker's tape measure is usually 60" (152.4cm) in length and can be rolled up and stored in your sewing box. It is perfect for taking body measurements and for other measuring that requires a flexible tool.

Water-Soluble Fabric Pen
These pens make temporary lines on fabric. The lines disappear when water is applied.

Tailor's Chalk
Tailor's chalk also makes temporary lines on fabric. It can be brushed away after use.

Hera Marker
A hera marker is a great alternative when pencils and chemical markers are not preferred. Simply trace the design with the hera marker, which leaves a fine crease or indentation in the fabric.

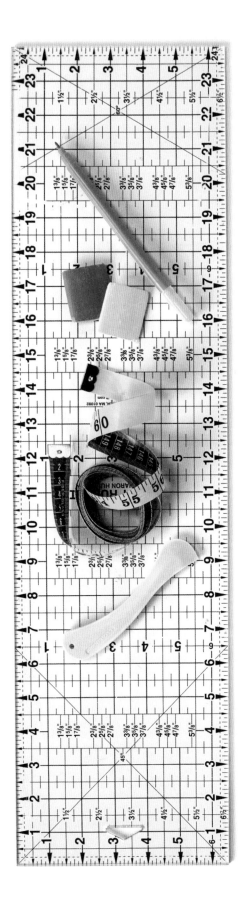

GENERAL TOOLS

Pins
Pins are invaluable for holding layers of fabric together while you sew and are essential for matching seams when sewing patchwork pieces together. Sharp pins with glass or plastic heads are preferred and can be easy to spot if dropped.

Pincushion
A pincushion is essential for holding your pins and needles close at hand. The *Cathedral Window Pincushion* in this book is both pretty and practical.

Wonder Clips
Wonder clips are a great alternative to pins and can securely hold multiple layers of fabric. They are particularly useful when stitching bias binding onto quilts and other projects.

Safety Pins
Safety pins are used to hold the layers of a quilted project together while quilting. Quilters' curved safety pins are easy to use.

Needles
To complete the projects in this book, you will need a few types of hand-sewing needles. Sharps are good general-purpose needles for stitching openings closed, appliqué, etc. You will also need embroidery needles, which have a larger eye for threading embroidery floss. Sashiko needles are longer and thicker than embroidery needles, and they're used for sashiko stitching. If you do not have any sashiko needles, embroidery needles will also work.

Seam Ripper
A seam ripper is a handy tool to help with unpicking crooked seams or removing unwanted threads from your work.

Compass
A compass is a drawing instrument used to draw circles and arcs. It's useful when drawing circles for appliqué or quilting designs.

EMBELLISHING TOOLS AND NOTIONS

Bias Tape Maker
Bias tape is available from sewing supply stores. You can easily make your own bias tape using fabric that coordinates with your project. A bias tape maker is a great tool to help you make perfect bias tape every time.

Snap Press
When attaching plastic or metal snaps to your project, you will need a snap-setting tool or snap press to securely attach the snaps. A snap press is a good investment if you make a lot of items with snap closures. The tool professionally attaches snaps in an instant.

Paper Piecing Hexagons
Precut paper shapes for English paper piecing are available from quilt shops and online stores. They're accurate and easy to use, and they save time when paper piecing. The shapes can be reused and come in a variety of sizes and shapes, including hexagons, diamonds, Dresden plates, etc.

FINISHING TOOLS

Iron
A good iron is invaluable when sewing. It's important to press the fabric prior to cutting and during each stage of construction. When choosing an iron, it's a good idea to find one with a steam function you can turn on and off, as well as an automatic shutoff function.

Pressing Cloth
A chemically treated pressing cloth, or Rajah cloth, is used when pressing pleats or when you need a crisp, professionally pressed surface.

Appliqué Mat
Teflon appliqué mats prevent fusible web from sticking to your iron when fusing appliqué pieces. These are a must to protect your iron and your project from sticky marks.

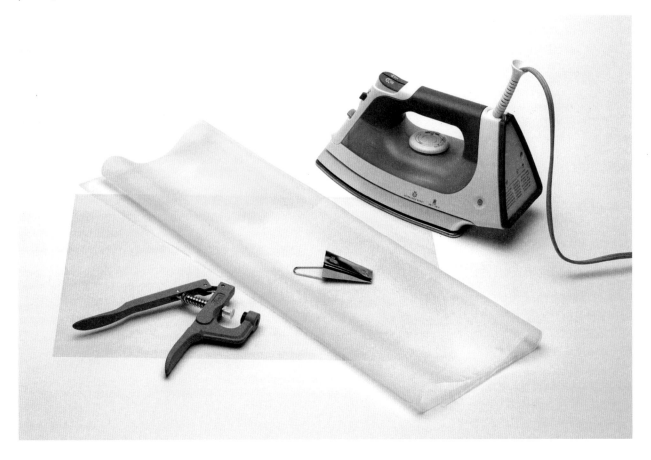

MATERIALS

Fabric

By selecting fabrics to suit your style, you can put your own creative touch on your next sewing project. There's a wide range of fabrics available in fabric shops and online, so you'll certainly be able to find something that appeals to you. Alternatively, check out thrift stores for used clothing and linens that can be repurposed in your next sewing project. The types of fabric you will need for the projects in this book include the following items:

* Cotton fabric (such as quilting cotton, linen and linen/cotton blends) is suitable for most of the projects in this book. It's easy to sew and has minimal shrinkage when laundered. Most of these projects use small quantities of fabric such as fat quarters (these usually measure 18" × 22" [45.7cm × 55.9cm]). Precut fabrics (such as charm squares, layer cakes or fat quarter bundles) will give you a wide variety of fabric for your fabric stash. When selecting fabrics, it's recommended that you choose a variety of colors and designs. Good basic fabrics to have in your stash include solids, polka dots, ginghams, stripes, geometrics and florals. Small-scale prints also work well for the projects in this book.

* Home décor-weight cotton is a thicker cotton fabric that is more tightly woven and heavier weight than quilting cotton.

* Lawn is a fine cotton fabric with a high thread count that gives it a silky feel. Liberty Fabrics specializes in high-quality cotton lawn.

* Felt is available in a wide range of colors in both wool and acrylic varieties. Wool felt is preferred and is much nicer to work with. One of the lovely features of felt is that it does not fray. Precut felt shapes such as circles are available on eBay and Etsy.

Thread

* **Sewing Thread:** Ideally, try to match the thread type to the fabric (cotton thread with cotton fabric, polyester thread with synthetic fabric, etc). Generally, the thread should be matched in color to the fabric unless you want contrasting thread to be a design feature. When it comes to thread, it's best to buy a good brand because cheap threads may break or result in lint buildup in your machine.

* **Embroidery Thread:** For the embroidery projects, stranded embroidery thread has been specified and the number of strands used is listed in the instructions.

* **Perle Cotton Thread:** Perle thread is made from cotton fibers that are double mercerized, which gives it a beautiful sheen. Perle thread is available in different thicknesses. Perle 5 is used for the chicken scratch embroidery projects. If you are unable to find perle cotton, use six strands of embroidery thread instead.

* **Sashiko Thread:** Traditional sashiko thread is 100% cotton, is loosely twisted and has a heavier look than regular quilting thread. It doesn't have a sheen like embroidery thread or perle cotton, and it's not intended to be separated into strands. If you're unable to find sashiko thread, you can use either embroidery thread or perle cotton thread.

Batting

Batting is used in quilts and some patchwork projects to add a layer between the top of the project and the backing. Cotton batting, either natural or white, is recommended for the projects in this book. Small quantities or offcuts will work well in these small projects.

Fusible Fleece

Thin and felt-like, fusible fleece is often used behind stitching projects to stabilize the fabric. It's available from brands such as Parlan and Pellon, and is also known as fusible wadding.

Fusible Web

Fusible web is used in raw-edge appliqué and melts when heated. It is placed between two layers of fabric. The melting action results in the fabrics becoming fused. It helps to reduce fraying and stabilizes the appliqué.

Embellishments

Ribbons, trims, leather patches and decorative cords are readily available at sewing stores and online, and they're great for customizing a project. Look for vintage trims in flea markets and thrift shops.

Flex Frames

These frames pop open when you squeeze the sides together and snap shut again when you release them. They're great to use in purses and are available in a range of sizes. You can find them on Etsy. They are also known as pinch frames or pouch frames.

TECHNIQUES

Here's a handy guide to the basic sewing and embellishing techniques used in the construction of the projects in this book. If you're a visual learner and you feel you need additional help, you may consider taking a craft class or checking out an online video tutorial for a demonstration of the technique. Alternatively, ask a crafty friend or relative for help or join a craft group with members who can show you the basics.

ESSENTIAL TECHNIQUES

Fabric Care

✳ Store your fabrics away from direct sunlight and dust. Suggested storage is inside a cupboard or in plastic tubs.

✳ Keep your fabric neatly folded and sorted (fabric can be sorted according to color, style, fabric designer, etc). Find a system that works for you.

✳ Some sewists like to prewash their fabric before use to prevent finished items from shrinking. If you think a fabric might shrink or bleed, prewash it in cold water. Precut fabrics (such as charm squares) should not be prewashed.

Cutting Fabrics

✳ When using an acrylic quilter's ruler and your rotary cutter, always cut away from you and retract the blade when not in use.

✳ Before you begin cutting your fabric, make sure the edge you are cutting from is straight. Ensuring the grain is straight will give the best results in sewing and patchwork. First, place the fabric on your cutting mat so the selvage (the printed edge of the fabric) is aligned with a horizontal grid line. Check the raw edge of the fabric to ensure it's aligned with a vertical grid line. If not, trim the fabric edge to square it up (Figure 1).

Figure 1

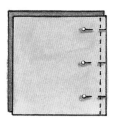

Figure 2

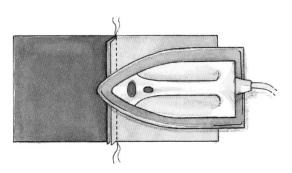

Figure 3

SEWING TECHNIQUES

Simple Piecing/Patchwork

✳ A ¼" (6mm) seam allowance is standard for patchwork. Check the specific instructions for the project you are working on. A ¼" (6mm) sewing machine foot makes accurate piecing easy.

✳ Pinning fabrics together, especially at seam junctions, makes all the difference to perfect patchwork seams. For small projects like the ones in this book, pin approximately 1½"–2" (3.8cm × 5.1cm) apart, ensuring raw edges are perfectly aligned, and all patchwork seams line up (Figure 2).

✳ Press the seams on one patchwork unit in the opposite direction of its neighboring unit so the seams will fit together neatly. Where possible, press toward the darker fabric so the seam allowance is less visible from the front (Figure 3).

Raw-Edge Appliqué

✳ Trace the design onto the paper backing side of the fusible web (Figure 4-A). Cut out the web, leaving a clearance of approximately ¼" (6mm) around the outside (Figure 4-B). Place the sticky side of the web on the wrong side of the fabric and iron the fabric to fuse the web following the manufacturer's instructions (Figure 4-C). Cut out the shape along the traced line using scissors (Figure 4-D). Remove the paper backing and fuse the web to the backing fabric (Figure 4-E).

✳ To stitch down the appliqué, use black thread in your sewing machine and a small straight stitch. Stitch around the edge, approximately ⅛" (3mm) in from the edge of the shape (Figure 4-F). Stitch two to three times around the edge to outline and ensure the appliqué is firmly attached. Vary the placement of the needle slightly to give a sketchy appearance.

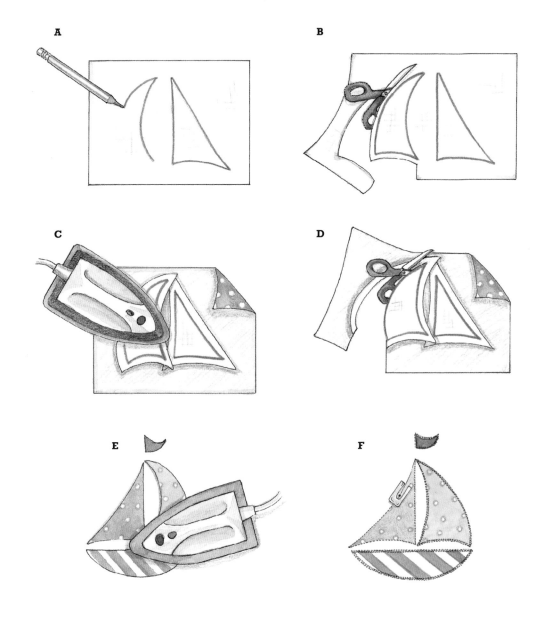

Figure 4

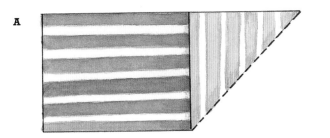

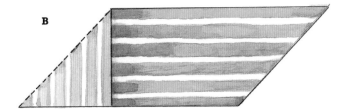

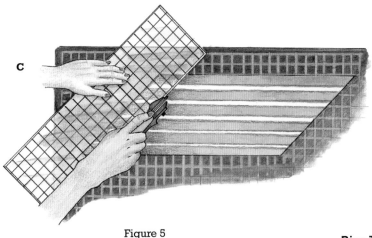

Figure 5

Cutting on the Bias

✳ Cutting strips on the bias helps you to bind a curved piece. To make bias strips, you must ensure the strips are cut on a 45° angle. Fold the fabric so the straight cut along the cross grain is parallel to the selvage of the fabric and forms a right-angle triangle (Figure 5-A). Cut the fabric along the fold line to establish your bias line (Figure 5-B). Use your first cut as a measuring guide as you cut the required number of bias strips (Figure 5-C).

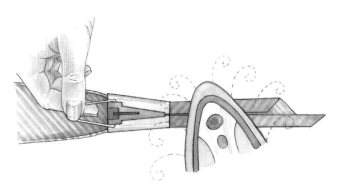

Figure 6

Bias Tape Maker

✳ Premade bias tape is available at most sewing and craft stores. Making your own tape means you can use the perfect printed fabric to suit your project. Small scale prints work best. You will need a bias tape maker (such as those made by Clover); they come in a variety of sizes, creating perfect bias tape of different widths. Follow the instructions on your bias tape maker and cut bias strips of the correct width. Insert the cut fabric through the tape maker. Pin the end of the fabric to your ironing board, then pull the tape maker while ironing the folded fabric. The bias tape is now ready to be used in sewing projects. Bias tape is best for sewing around curves (Figure 6).

✳ If you're binding a straight edge, it's not necessary to use bias binding. Instead, create binding from strips cut on the straight grain. Fold the strip in half and press.

Attach Binding With Mitered Corners

✯ On the right side of the project, lay the end of the binding down and line up the raw edge of the binding with the raw edge of the project. Pin the binding in place up to the corner. Sew through all layers using a ¼" (6mm) seam allowance. Stop sewing ¼" (6mm) away from the corner edge, and back tack. To form the mitered corner, fold the binding at a right angle from the quilt to form an angled fold. Fold it back down along the raw edge of the adjoining side, aligning the raw edges as you did on the previous side. Sew it in place until you are ¼" (6mm) from the next corner. Repeat until all sides are bound (Figure 7).

✯ Fold the binding over the edge of the project from front to back and pin in place so the folded edge on the back covers the stitching line. Hand-stitch in place to secure.

Quilting

✯ Quilts and small quilted projects, as featured in this book, are assembled with three layers: the top (which may be patchwork), the batting and the backing. Low-loft cotton batting is recommended. The three layers should be pressed and smooth. Hold the layers together with either safety pins or quilt basting spray.

✯ Quilting is the method used for sewing the three layers together. This can be done by hand or by machine. The projects in this book have been machine quilted. If your sewing machine does not have a built-in dual feed for quilting, a walking foot is recommended to ensure the layers feed through the machine evenly and there is no puckering.

✯ Most of the projects are quilted with straight-line quilting. To ensure perfectly straight lines, mark the stitching lines with masking tape or use a hera marker.

✯ Increase your stitch length to 3.0 to 3.5 for machine quilting.

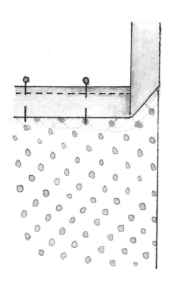
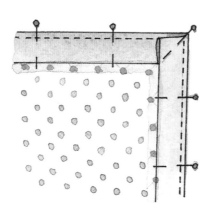
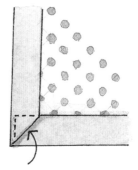

Figure 7

ENGLISH PAPER PIECING

* English paper piecing is the technique of hand-piecing fabric over paper templates to create a variety of shapes, most commonly hexagons and diamonds. They are quick to baste and fit together perfectly. English paper piecing is a great portable project to sew on the go.

* Print and cut a number of templates from thick paper or lightweight card stock, or use precut templates (available from quilt stores).

* Place the templates on the wrong side of the fabric and cut around each, leaving a ¼"–⅜" (6mm–1cm) seam allowance on all sides.

* Fold the seam allowance on one side over the edge of the template and press in place using a finger presser, hera marker or your fingers. Secure it in place using a paper clip or wonder clip. Beginning at the corner to the left of the paper clip, fold down the seam allowance on the next side and take a small stitch (picking up only one or two threads of the fabric) across the fold to secure. Continue working your way counter-clockwise around the hexagon, folding down the seam allowance on each corner and securing the fold in place with a couple of stitches at each fold (Figure 8-A). Try to keep as close as possible to the folded edge. Continue until you have the required number of hexagons prepared. Do not stitch or pin through the paper. Carefully remove the paper clip. Press well on the back for a crisp edge.

* Leave the papers in place when you are joining seven hexagons to form a flower. Start by joining the six outer hexagons into a ring. Place two hexagons together with the right sides facing. Join them together along one edge with a whipstitch, being careful to pick up only a few threads of the fabric and to avoid stitching through the paper (Figure 8-B). Continue attaching one hexagon at a time until six hexagons form a ring. Hand-stitch the remaining hexagon into the center of the flower using the same technique (Figure 8-C). Carefully remove the papers and press them for reuse. Press the back of the hexagon flower (Figure 8-D).

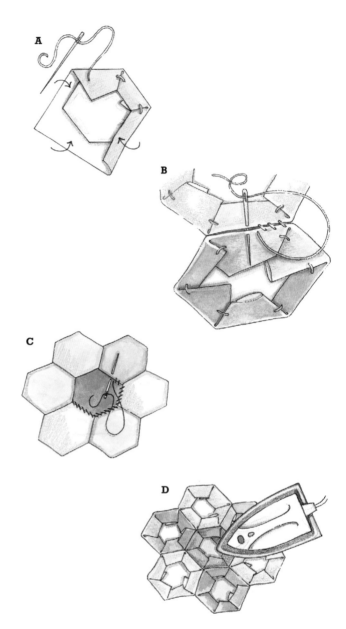

Figure 8

TIP

Use silk thread or a finer thread, such as 50-weight thread, to attach the hexagons so the stitching is nearly invisible.

EMBROIDERY TECHNIQUES

Adding simple hand-stitched details can really make a home-sewn project your own. Hand sewing and embroidery are relaxing and fun to do in front of the television, when traveling or when in a waiting room.

Basic Hand Stitches

✱ There are a wide range of embroidery stitches, but the basic stitches shown below are all you need for most of the projects in this book (Figures 9–14). Feel free to substitute your own favorite hand-stitching and embroidery details.

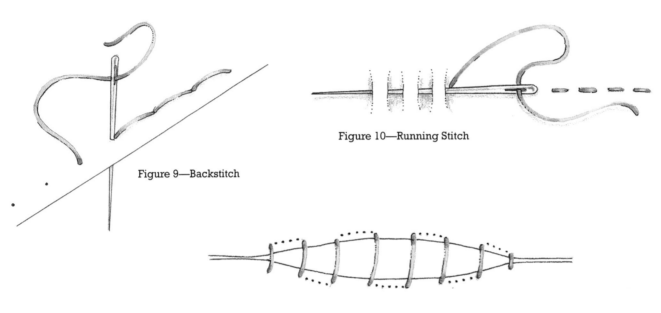

Figure 9—Backstitch

Figure 10—Running Stitch

Figure 11—Ladder Stitch

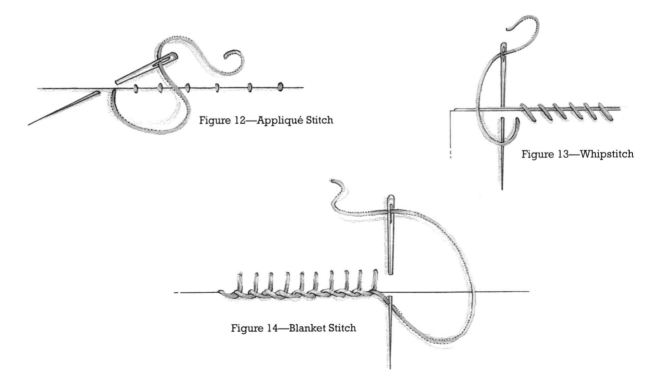

Figure 12—Appliqué Stitch

Figure 13—Whipstitch

Figure 14—Blanket Stitch

Chicken Scratch

✳ Chicken scratch embroidery is a variation of cross-stitch that is traditionally stitched on gingham fabric using perle mercerized cotton thread or stranded embroidery thread. The gingham squares act as stitching guides and help to form a lacy pattern.

✳ First, prepare the gingham by pressing some fusible interfacing to the wrong side of the fabric. Use an embroidery hoop to help maintain even tension as you stitch. Work the cross-stitch, then add the woven details to the embroidery.

✳ These are the basic stitches used in chicken scratch embroidery:

* Cross-stitch (Figure 15)
* Woven Square – Four Corners (Figure 16)
* Woven Oval – Two Corners (Figure 17)

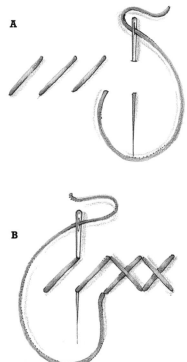

A

B

Figure 15

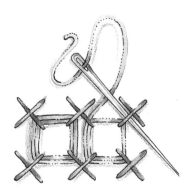

Figure 16

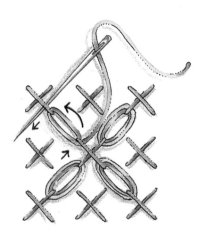

Figure 17

Sashiko

* Sashiko is a form of decorative reinforcement stitching that originated in Japan as a method to repair worn clothing. Sashiko running stitch is now used as decorative stitching in quilts, home décor items and clothing. Designs are often geometric with repeating patterns.

* Begin by tracing your design onto the fabric using your preferred method of tracing (pattern transfer paper works well for dark fabrics). Sashiko stitches are always longer on the top of the fabric than on the underside. The ratio is typically 3:1, meaning the underside is one-third the length of the top stitch (Figure 18).

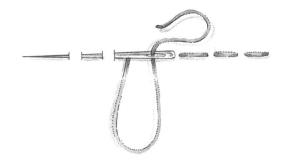

Figure 18

CROCHET

✳ Crochet terms vary throughout the world, which can cause some confusion. This book uses U.S. terms for the crochet stitches.

✳ A few projects in this book incorporate basic crochet. The stitches you will need to know are illustrated below and on the following pages (Figures 19–24).

Figure 19—Chain

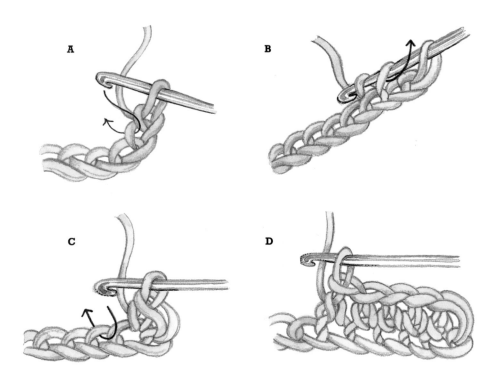

Figure 20—Single Crochet

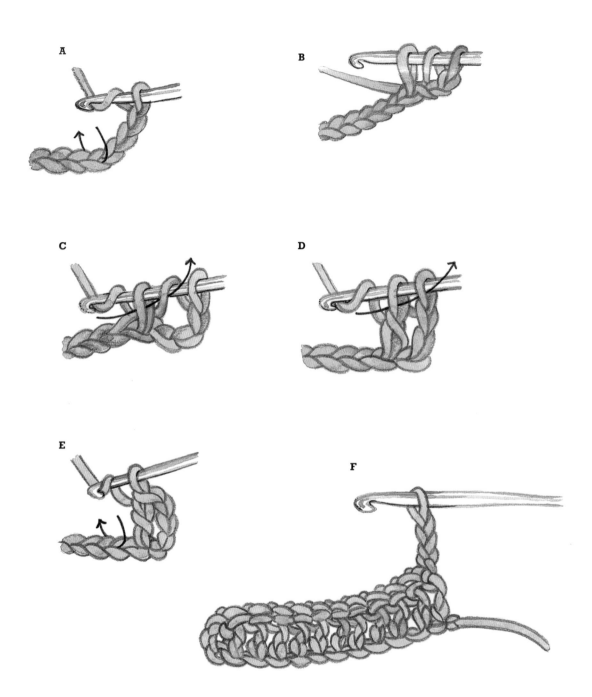

Figure 21—Double Crochet

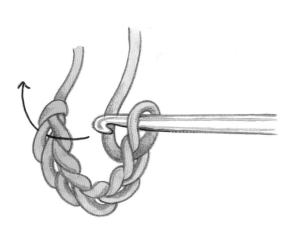

Figure 22—Crochet Circle

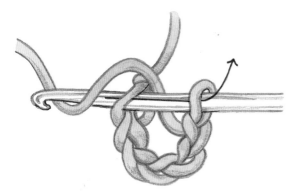

Figure 23—Slip Stitch (to close the circle)

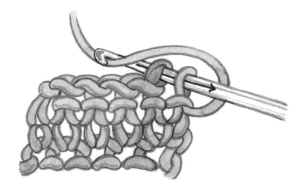

Figure 24—End a Row

CHAPTER 1

Home

Decorating your home with stylish and practical handmade items is the perfect way to showcase your creative flair and add a welcoming touch. Your personality and style will be reflected in the fabrics you use. Whether your style is modern, retro or traditional, you are bound to find some projects to inspire you among the *Bonjour Paris Doorstop*, *Retro Pillow*, *Kyoto Placemats* and *Crisscross Coasters*. These projects make great gifts for friends and family to celebrate a housewarming, birthday or other special occasion.

Bonjour Paris Doorstop

DIFFICULTY
★ ★ ☆

FINISHED SIZE
7" (17.8cm) in height, excluding the handle
6" (15.2cm) wide at its base

Hold your door open or closed in style with this Parisian-inspired doorstop. Made from printed linen with a Parisian theme and coordinating quilting cotton, it features Eiffel Tower silhouette appliqués and a ribbon accent. It is quick to construct and could be easily customized with an appliqué motif of your choice (or omit the appliqué for a more contemporary doorstop).

MATERIALS

3 fat quarters of quilting cotton or linen in low-volume polka-dot print (Fabric A), Parisian-themed fabric (Fabric B) for sides and gingham (Fabric C) for top and bottom of doorstop

Two 5" × 7" (12.7cm × 17.8cm) rectangles of cotton fabric for Eiffel Tower appliqué

Fusible web for Eiffel Tower appliqué

6" (15cm) zipper

7½" (19cm) length of 1¼" (3.2cm) wide cotton webbing for handle

4" (10.2cm) of ¾" (1.9cm) wide striped ribbon for the ribbon accent

Polyester fiber filling (or your stuffing of choice)

3 cups of rice, dried beans or stuffing pellets

Resealable plastic bag

TOOLS & SUPPLIES

Basic sewing tools (see Tools and Materials)

Appliqué mat (optional)

TEMPLATES

Top Panel, Side Panel, Bottom Panel, Eiffel Tower Appliqué (on CD)

Note: All seam allowances are ½" (1.3cm) unless otherwise indicated.

CUTTING AND PREPARING FABRICS

Using the templates, cut

- 2 side panels from the low-volume polka-dot print for appliqué background (Fabric A)
- 2 side panels from the Parisian-themed fabric (Fabric B)
- 1 top panel from the navy gingham (Fabric C)

From Fabric C, cut

- One 7" × 4" (17.8cm × 10.2cm) rectangle
- One 7" × 5" (17.8cm × 12.7cm) rectangle

    (These pieces will be trimmed using the bottom panel template after the zipper has been installed).

Referring to the templates, transfer the pattern markings to the fabric.

EIFFEL TOWER APPLIQUÉS

1 Using the template, trace 2 Eiffel Tower designs onto the paper side of the fusible web, at least ½" (1.3cm) apart. Cut around the designs leaving at least a ¼" (6mm) margin around all edges.

2 Following the manufacturer's instructions, fuse the web onto the wrong side of the 2 fabrics you are using for the Eiffel Tower appliqués. Cut along the traced lines. Center an Eiffel Tower onto one of the side panels and fuse it. Repeat for the other Eiffel Tower.

3 Edgestitch around the Eiffel Tower silhouettes using black thread to secure them to the side panels. Stitch around each shape 3 times. Try to vary the stitching line so it has a slightly sketchy appearance.

ATTACH THE HANDLE

4 Fold the ribbon in half. Stitch through both layers of the ribbon ¾" (1.9cm) from the raw edge so it creates a ribbon loop. Turn the ribbon right-side out so the stitching is on the inside. Thread the loop of ribbon over one end of the webbing. Position it in place 1½" (3.8cm) from one end. Stitch it onto the webbing to secure.

5 Mark the midpoint of 2 opposite sides of the top panel of the doorstop. Pin both ends of the webbing to the midpoints of the top panel so the edges are aligned. Baste in place using a ¼" (6mm) seam allowance and stitch over the ends a few times for reinforcement (Figure 1).

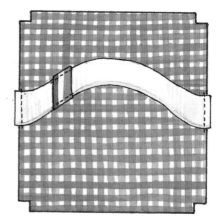

Figure 1

INSERT THE ZIPPER

6 Using the 7" × 4" (17.8cm × 10.2cm) rectangle, align one of the long edges along the bottom edge of the zipper so the right sides are facing and the edges are aligned. Stitch the zipper to the fabric using a ¼" (6mm) seam (Figure 2). Press the fabric so the right side is facing up (Figure 3).

7 Using the 7" × 5" (17.8cm × 12.7cm) rectangle, fold down 1" (2.5cm) along the long edge and press. Align the long edge that's closest to the fold along the top edge of the zipper so the right sides are facing and the edges are aligned. Stitch the zipper to the fabric using a ¼" (6mm) seam (Figure 4). Position the bottom panel with the fabric right-side up. Fold the fabric above the zipper down along the fold line so the fold of fabric hides the zipper from view. Baste along the side edges to hold the fold in place. Stitch a line across the panel through all layers, ¾" (1.9cm) above the fold line (Figure 5).

8 Pin the bottom panel template to the bottom panel with the zipper centered and trim the fabric to fit.

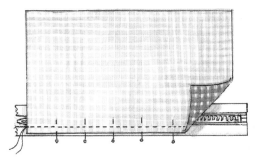

Figure 2

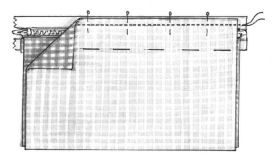

Figure 3

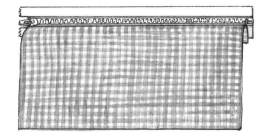

Figure 4

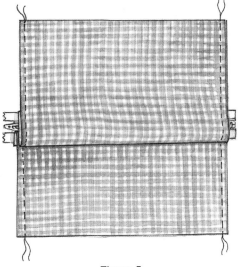

Figure 5

ASSEMBLE THE DOORSTOP

9 With right sides together, align the top edge of a side panel with a side of the top, matching pattern markings. Pin in place. Stitch along the stitching line between the dots as marked (Figure 6).

10 Repeat for all 4 sides of the top panel, ensuring Fabric A pieces are on opposite sides of the top panel (Figure 7).

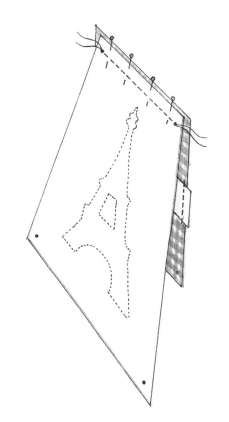

Figure 6

Figure 7

11 With right sides together, pin side seams, matching the pattern markings. Sew the side panels together, stitching from the top to the bottom between the dots (Figure 8).

12 With right sides together, pin the bottom panel to the doorstop, matching the pattern markings. Stitch around all 4 sides of the bottom panel. Leave the zipper open while attaching the bottom panel (Figure 9).

13 Turn the doorstop right-side out through the zipper opening. Press.

14 Place a sandwich bag inside the doorstop and fill it with rice or other weighted stuffing. Seal up the bag and position it so it's flat at the base of the doorstop. Check to see if the doorstop is heavy enough for your purposes. If not, add another sandwich bag with weighted filling.

15 Add polyester fiber filling to the top section of the doorstop above the rice, until it is stuffed as desired.

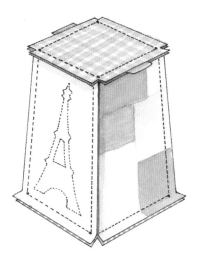

Figure 8

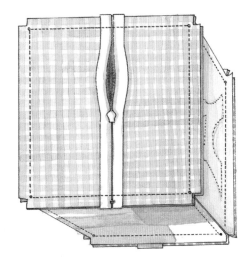

Figure 9

TIP

Use a small jug to pour the rice into the sandwich bag.

Retro Pillow

DIFFICULTY
★ ★ ★

FINISHED SIZE
18" (45.7cm) square, excluding the crocheted edge

This vintage-style pillow is constructed from hexagons cut from 1930s reproduction fabrics and features a colorful crocheted shell edging. Perfect for the living room or bedroom, this pillow is bright and cheerful. The hexagons are machine-sewn, which makes for quick construction. It has a zipper closure in the back.

ABBREVIATIONS

sl st: slip stitch
ch: chain
sc: single crochet
dc: double crochet

MATERIALS

22 fabric scraps in red, blue, green and yellow, each measuring at least 6" (15.2cm) square (alternatively, use precut hexagons in a Honeycomb pack)

⅔ yard (61cm) of black printed quilting cotton in a typography print for the pillow backing

18" (45cm) black zipper

1 skein of 4-ply crochet cotton in red

18" (45cm) pillow form

TOOLS & SUPPLIES

Basic sewing tools (see Tools and Materials)

Crochet hook size C or D (2.75mm or 3.25mm)

Tapestry needle

TEMPLATES

Hexagon (on CD)

Note: All seam allowances are ¼" (6mm) unless otherwise noted.

CUTTING AND PREPARING FABRICS

Cut 22 hexagons from the assorted fabric scraps using the template provided (or use precut Honeycomb hexagons, which measure 6" [15.2cm] from one tip to the tip on the opposite side).

Using a water-soluble fabric marker, mark a dot at each corner of the hexagon where indicated on the template.

From the backing fabric, cut

- One 19" (48.3cm) square
- One 19" × 3" (48.3cm × 7.6cm) strip

FRONT OF PILLOW

1 Lay out the hexagons as shown in Figure 1 so you have 5 vertical columns of hexagons. The first, third and fifth columns will have 4 hexagons, and the second and fourth columns will have 5 hexagons.

2 Starting with column 1, sew the first 2 hexagons together with the right sides facing, stitching between the dots as marked on the fabric. Backstitch at the beginning and end of the seam. Add each hexagon in the column until they are all connected. Repeat for each of the columns. Finger press the seams open but do not press with the iron at this stage. Reduce the stitch length to 2 to make it easier to start and stop on the dots (Figure 2).

3 Sew the columns together by positioning column 1 on top of column 2 and aligning the first side. Carefully sew between the dots as marked, pushing the seam allowance out of the way. At the end of each side, open the seam and check that the fabric hasn't puckered. Continue sewing the remainder of the sides until column 2 is attached (Figure 3).

4 Continue to sew the columns together, one side at a time, until the pillow top is completed.

5 Gently press all of the seams open, then press the front of the pillow top.

6 Trim the pillow top so that it's 19" (48.3cm) square. Set aside.

TIP

If you don't like to crochet, how about using some colorful pom-pom trim as the edging?

Figure 1

Figure 2

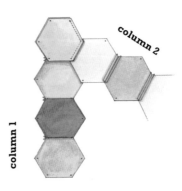

Figure 3

BACK OF PILLOW

7 Lay out the large backing square on a flat surface with the right side facing up. Press under 1½" (3.8cm) along the bottom edge. This will become a placket that hides the zipper. Unfold the fabric and lay it flat. Place the zipper right-side down along the right-side raw edge of the fabric with the zipper pull on the left-hand side. Pin in place. Refold the placket. Stitch the zipper in place through both layers of fabric (Figure 4).

8 Pin the bottom edge of the zipper to the 19" × 3" (48.3cm × 7.6cm) backing strip with right sides facing and stitch in place. Press. Topstitch close to the seam.

9 Lay the backing piece out flat so the placket covers the zipper. Trim the backing piece to 19" (48.3cm) square.

10 Lay the backing piece on top of the pillow front with the right sides facing and the zipper partially open. Pin around the outside of the pillow. Stitch around the pillow using a ½" (1.3cm) seam allowance. Clip the corners. Turn the pillow right-side out through the opening in the zipper. Press.

11 Topstitch around the outside of the pillow using a ⅜" (1cm) seam allowance.

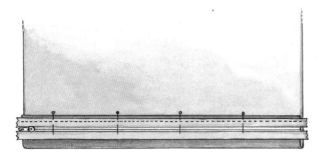

Figure 4

CROCHET SHELL EDGING

12 Cut a length of crochet cotton that is 7½ yards (6.9m) long. This will be long enough to blanket stitch around half of the pillow. Thread the yarn onto a tapestry needle. Tie both ends together. You will blanket stitch around the outside of the pillow to form the foundation for the crochet.

13 Using a water-soluble fabric pen, mark dots around the outside of the pillow at ½" (1.3cm) intervals. Starting at one corner, bring the needle inside the pillow and out the front of the pillow at one corner. Blanket stitch around the outside of the pillow using stitches that are ⅜" (1cm) in length and spaced ½" (1.3cm) apart where marked. When you get to the diagonal corner, tie off the yarn. Rethread the needle with another 7½ yards (6.9m) of yarn and make a blanket stitch around the remainder of the pillow. Tie off the thread (place the ends inside the pillow cover).

14 Crochet the shell edging around the pillow as follows:

> **Row 1:** Join with a sl st. Ch 2, 2 sc in the first blanket stitch space, *3 sc in the next blanket stitch space;* repeat from * to * until each blanket stitch space has been filled. Sl st into the second chain from the beginning.

> **Row 2:** Ch 1, sc in the beginning stitch, sc in the next stitch, *skip 2 sts, 7 dc in the next st, skip 2 sts, sc in the next 2 sts;* repeat from * to * until you reach the end of the pillow. Finish with a sc. Tie off.

15 Weave in the loose ends of cotton yarn. Insert the pillow form into the pillow cover.

Kyoto Placemat

DIFFICULTY
★ ★ ☆

FINISHED SIZE
18" × 12½" (45.7cm × 31.8cm)

These modern placemats feature a panel of traditional Japanese sashiko embroidery stitched on linen and combined with modern organic cotton prints. Mix and match the fabrics and colors to make a fun table setting to go with your noodle bowls.

MATERIALS (makes 1 placemat)

Fat quarter of linen for sashiko stitching

Fat quarter of feature fabric for placemat center

Fat quarter of contrasting fabric for placemat side panel

Fat quarter of contrasting fabric for placemat backing

Fat quarter of fusible fleece

1 skein of sashiko thread (or use perle 5 or embroidery thread)

TOOLS & SUPPLIES

Basic sewing tools (see Tools and Materials)

Sashiko needle

Pattern transfer (carbon) paper for tracing pattern

Embroidery hoop (optional)

TEMPLATES

Sashiko Design (on CD)

Note: All seam allowances are ½" (1.3cm), unless otherwise indicated.

CUTTING AND PREPARING FABRICS

From the fabrics, cut

- One 5½" × 13½" (14cm × 34.3cm) strip from the linen
- One 11½" × 13½" (29.2cm × 34.3cm) rectangle from the feature fabric
- One 4" × 13½" (10.2cm × 34.3cm) strip from the contrasting fabric
- One 19" × 13½" (48.3cm × 34.3cm) rectangle from the backing fabric
- One 18" × 12½" (45.7cm × 31.8cm) rectangle from the fusible fleece

SASHIKO STITCHING

1 Trace the sashiko design onto the center of the linen strip using pattern transfer paper or your preferred transfer method. Cut a length of sashiko thread and stitch the design (refer to Sashiko in Embroidery Techniques). Press the completed stitchery.

SASHIKO

Sashiko is a traditional Japanese embroidery technique that consists of a series of running stitches in geometric and repetitive designs. The stitching was used to patch worn clothing and to stitch layers of cloth together for warmth and durability.

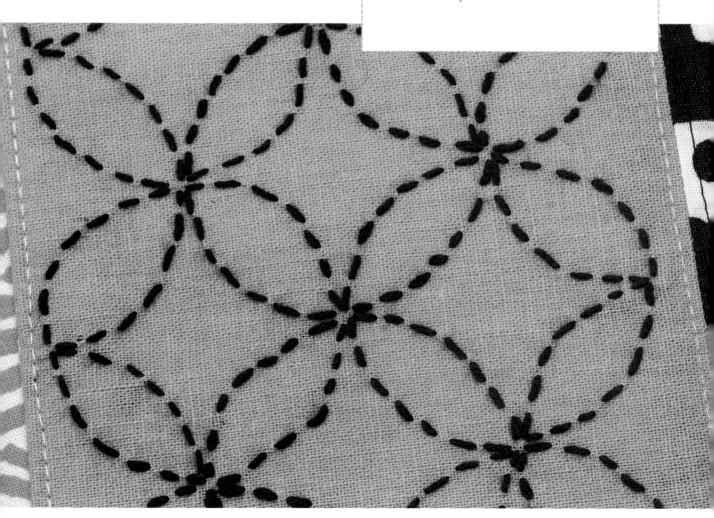

ASSEMBLE PLACEMAT FRONT

2 Position the placemat center so that it's flat on your work surface and right-side up. Place the sashiko stitching right-side down on the left side of the center panel so that the edges are aligned along the left side and at the top and bottom. Pin in place. Stitch together using a ½" (1.3cm) seam allowance. Position the orange side panel so that it's face down on the right of the placemat center fabric with the right edge, top and bottom aligned. Stitch both pieces together. Press the seams flat. Topstitch along both sides of both seams using a scant ⅛" (3mm) seam allowance. Center the fusible fleece on the back of the placemat front and press to fuse it into position.

ASSEMBLE PLACEMAT

3 Position the placemat front on a flat surface with the right side facing upward. Position the placemat backing on top with the right sides facing and the edges aligned. Pin both layers together. Stitch around the outside of the placemat, leaving a 5" (12.7cm) gap on one long side for turning. Clip the corners. Turn out the placemat through the gap in the lining. Press the placemat. Hand-stitch the gap in the side closed. Edgestitch around the outside of the placemat.

Crisscross Coasters

DIFFICULTY
★ ☆ ☆

FINISHED SIZE
4½" (11.4cm) diameter, excluding rickrack edging

Colorful patchwork crosses are combined with a low-volume background and rickrack trim, in these *Crisscross Coasters*. Colorful and practical, they're perfectly sized to protect your table from hot coffee cups and icy cold drinks. This is a great project to help you master simple patchwork and sewing in a curved line. Ideal for using scraps of fabric and trim, these coasters also make a useful gift.

MATERIALS (makes a set of 4 coasters)

Fat quarter of low-volume typography cotton print on a white background

Fat quarter of black geometric print for coaster backing

Charm squares (or scraps measuring 5" [12.7cm] square) in 4 bright colors

½ yard (45.7cm) of rickrack trim in 4 colors (⅜" [1cm] wide)

Fat quarter of cotton batting

TOOLS & SUPPLIES

Basic sewing tools (see Tools and Materials)

Chopstick or turning tool

TEMPLATES

Circle (on CD)

Note: All seam allowances are ¼" (6mm) unless otherwise noted.

CUTTING AND PREPARING FABRICS

For each coaster, cut the following:

From the low-volume print, cut

- Two 5" × 1¼" (12.7cm × 3.2cm) rectangles
- Four 2¼" × 1½" (5.7cm × 3.8cm) rectangles
- Two 1¼" × 1½" (3.2cm × 3.8cm) rectangles

From the colored fabric, cut

- Two 1½" (3.8cm) squares
- One 3½" × 1½" (8.9cm × 3.8cm) rectangle

From the backing fabric, cut

- 1 circle using the template provided

From the batting, cut

- One 5" (12.7cm) square

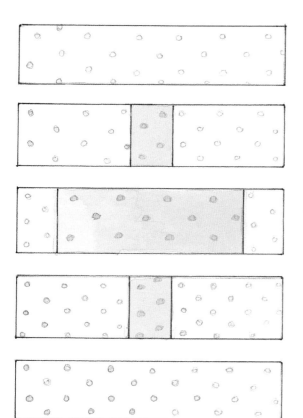

Figure 1

PATCHWORK CROSSES

1 Arrange the patchwork pieces into 5 rows to create a colored cross design (Figure 1). Beginning in row 2, place 2 adjoining patchwork pieces together with the right sides facing and the edges aligned. Pin the strip together along the short edge and stitch in place. Add the remaining piece of fabric and stitch it to the other side of the colored fabric. Press the seams towards the center. Repeat for rows 3 and 4. Press.

2 Arrange row 1 and 2 with the right sides facing and pin them in place along the long edge (Figure 2). Stitch row 1 to row 2. Press. Continue and add rows 3, 4 and 5. Press. You will now have a patchwork square measuring 5" (12.7cm) (Figure 3).

3 Layer the patchwork cross on top of the batting square. Pin the layers together. Stitch in the ditch around the outside of the cross through both layers.

4 Using the circle template and a water-soluble fabric pen, draw a circle on top of the patchwork cross. Cut along the line. Pin the rickrack around the outside edge of the circle, on the right side of the coaster, and stitch to secure.

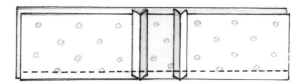

Figure 2

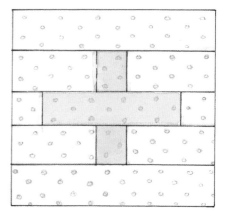

Figure 3

ASSEMBLE THE COASTER

5 Position the patchwork cross on top of the black backing fabric with the right sides facing. Pin this piece in place. Stitch around the outside of the circle, leaving a 1½" (3.8cm) gap for turning.

6 Clip around the curve but not through the stitching line. Carefully turn the coaster right-side out through the gap in the backing. Using a chopstick, make sure all the edges are turned out. Press. Tuck in the seam allowance around the gap and press again. Hand-sew the opening closed using a slipstitch. Topstitch around the outside of the coaster, close to the edge.

7 Repeat steps 1–6 to create 3 more coasters.

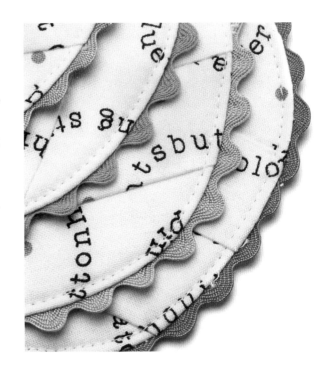

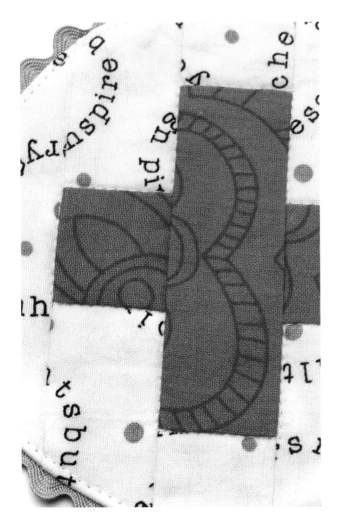

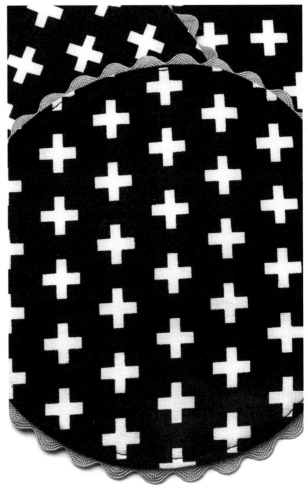

CHAPTER 2

Bedroom

Add some sweetness to your bedroom with homemade items that are both practical and pretty. Make a *Sweet Dreams Pillowcase* to sleep on, a *Pretty Patchwork Jewelry Wrap* to store your favorite jewelry, *Dress Form Lavender Sachets* for your closet or a *Grandmother's Flower Garden Dustcover* to keep your special garments dust-free. These projects make lovely gifts for special friends.

Sweet Dreams Pillowcase

DIFFICULTY
★ ☆ ☆

FINISHED SIZE
28¾" × 18½" (73cm × 47cm)

Add some vintage charm to your bedroom with a delightful pillowcase featuring a panel of chicken scratch embroidery. Team the gingham with a floral print and some fine quilter's muslin. Making a pillowcase is the perfect beginner's project!

MATERIALS

Fat quarter of mauve gingham fabric (woven or printed) with checks approx. ⁵⁄₁₆" (8mm) apart (for chicken scratch panel)

⅛ yard (11.4cm) of mauve printed floral quilter's cotton

¾ yard (68.6cm) of white quilter's muslin

¾ yard (68.6cm) of mauve printed quilter's cotton for pillowcase backing

1 skein of white perle 5 thread (1 ball is 49 yards [44.8m])

Fat quarter of fusible fleece (such as Pellon or Parlan)

TOOLS & SUPPLIES

Basic sewing tools (see Tools and Materials)

Embroidery needle and needle threader

Embroidery hoop

Serger (optional)

Note: All seam allowances are ¼" (6mm) unless otherwise noted.

CUTTING AND PREPARING FABRICS

From the fabrics, cut

- One 13" × 19" (33cm × 48.3cm) rectangle from the gingham fabric
- One 6½" × 19" (16.5cm × 48.3cm) rectangle from the fusible fleece
- One 3½" × 19" (8.9cm × 48.3cm) strip from the floral print
- One 19" × 23" (48.3cm × 58.4cm) rectangle from the quilter's muslin
- One 19" × 36½" (8.9cm × 92.7cm) rectangle from the printed cotton

CHICKEN SCRATCH PANEL

1 Press the gingham fabric in half lengthwise, with wrong sides together, so it measures 6½" × 19" (16.5cm × 48.3cm). Open the gingham fabric and fuse the fleece to the back so it covers half of the fabric, with the edges aligned on 3 sides.

2 Refer to Chicken Scratch in Embroidery Techniques (page 21). Work 5 rows of woven squares, each 28 columns across. Wrap the thread around each square 3 times. The chicken scratch panel will need to start 3 rows down from the folded edge and 3 columns across. If your gingham is not spaced ⁵⁄₁₆" (8mm) apart, start the stitching approximately ¾" (1.9cm) down and ¾" (1.9cm) across from the folded edge. The stitching should measure approximately 3½" × 17½" (8.9cm × 44.4cm) when complete. The chicken scratch panel is worked through one layer of the gingham fabric, on the half that has the fusible fleece. Press the gingham and fold so that the completed chicken scratch panel measures 6½" × 19" (16.5cm × 48.3cm).

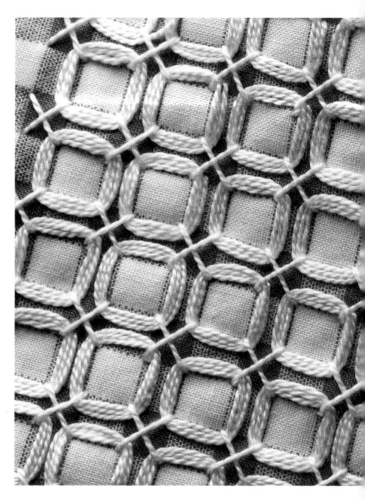

ASSEMBLE THE PILLOWCASE

3 Fold the floral fabric in half lengthwise and press it so it measures 1¾" × 19" (4.4cm × 48.3cm). Lay the gingham panel flat on a table with the embroidery facing up. Position the floral strip on top of the gingham panel so the raw edges are aligned. Pin them together and baste them in place (Figure 1).

4 Lay out the white muslin with the right side facing up. Place the gingham stitched panel on a short edge so the right sides are facing and the raw edges are aligned. Pin them in place. Stitch the panel to the pillowcase front. Serge the raw edges. Press the pillowcase front and topstitch ⅛" (3mm) from the seam.

5 Take the pillowcase backing. To create a hem, fold over ½" (1.3cm) along a short edge. Press. Fold under another ½" (1.3cm). Press and stitch in place.

6 Lay the pillowcase front on top of the pillowcase back with right sides facing and the short, unfinished edges aligned. Pin it in place. To create the flap, fold the hemmed edge of the pillowcase back over the chicken scratch panel. Pin it in place. Stitch along the 2 long sides and the short edge. Serge the raw edges. Turn the pillowcase right-side out and press it (Figure 2).

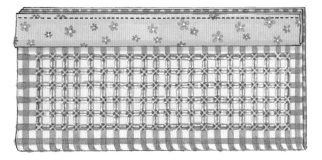

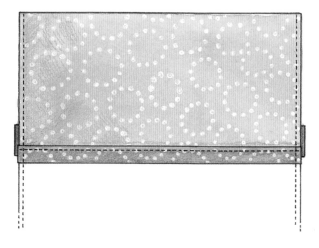

Figure 1

Figure 2

Grandmother's Flower Garden Dustcover

DIFFICULTY
★ ★ ★

FINISHED SIZE
11" × 21" (27.9cm × 53.3cm)

Protect your special outfits from dust settling across the shoulders with this clothing dustcover. It features a paper-pieced Grandmother's Flower Garden quilt block, which is a popular vintage quilt design.

MATERIALS

½ yard (45.7cm) of white or gray striped fabric for dust cover front

½ yard (45.7cm) pink polka-dot fabric for dustcover back

⅛ yard (11.4cm) floral print for edging

1 yard (0.9m) white quilter's muslin for lining

Scraps of 7 prints, measuring at least 3" (7.6cm) square for paper-pieced hexagons

Small fabric label or motif (optional)

TOOLS & SUPPLIES

Basic sewing tools (see Tools and Materials)

Card stock

TEMPLATES

Hexagon, Dustcover (on CD)

Note: All seam allowances are ½" (1.3cm), unless otherwise indicated.

CUTTING AND PREPARING FABRICS

Using the Dustcover template, cut out the following and transfer the pattern markings to each pattern piece:

- 1 dustcover panel from white or gray striped fabric
- 1 dustcover panel from pink polka-dot fabric
- 2 dustcover panels from white quilter's muslin

From the floral print, cut

- Two 2½ × 22" (6.3cm × 55.9cm) strips

PREPARE THE GRANDMOTHER'S FLOWER GARDEN BLOCK

1 Prepare 7 hexagons from the assorted prints. Refer to English Paper Piecing in the Techniques section.

2 Piece the 7 hexagons together to form a Grandmother's Flower Garden block.

3 Position the flower block so it's centered 2" (5.1cm) below the top of the dustcover's front panel. Hand-stitch in place to secure.

TIP

This is a great project for anyone who wants to try English paper piecing, which is a popular form of quilting dating back to the 1770s. Paper templates are used to ensure accuracy when piecing. When paper was scarce in early America, women used old letters and newspapers for their paper templates.

ADD A LABEL TO THE BACK OF THE DUSTCOVER (Optional)

4 Using fabric that features labels or motifs, cut out a small label, leaving a ¼" (6mm) seam allowance around the label. Press the seam allowance under the fabric. Position the label on the center of the back panel, approximately 1½" (3.8cm) below the top edge. Hand-stitch (or machine-stitch) in place.

ASSEMBLE THE DUSTCOVER

5 Lay the polka-dot backing on top of the front of the cover with the right sides facing and pin them together. Stitch from the bottom of the left side around to the bottom of the right side, leaving an opening along the top edge (between the pattern markings), and leaving the bottom edge open. Clip the curves. Press the seams open. Turn the dust cover right-side out.

6 Lay the 2 white lining pieces on top of each other and repeat step 5. The wrong side of the lining should be facing out.

7 Lay the 2 floral strips on top of each other with right sides facing and edges aligned. Stitch across both short edges to form a loop. Fold the loop in half lengthwise and press it. Pin the floral loop around the bottom edge of the dustcover with right sides facing, matching the side seams and the raw edges. Baste in place using a ⅛" (3mm) seam allowance (Figure 1).

8 Place the lining over the dustcover so the right sides are facing. Match the side seams. Stitch around the bottom edge using a ¼" (6mm) seam allowance.

9 Carefully turn the dustcover right-side out through the opening at the top. Press the cover. Hand-stitch the lining to the dustcover around the top opening using a slip stitch. Be sure not to stitch the hanger opening shut while attaching the lining.

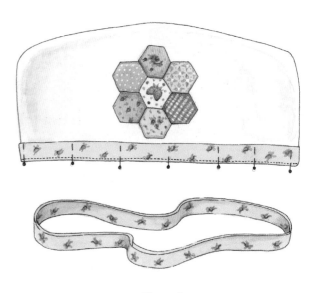

Figure 1

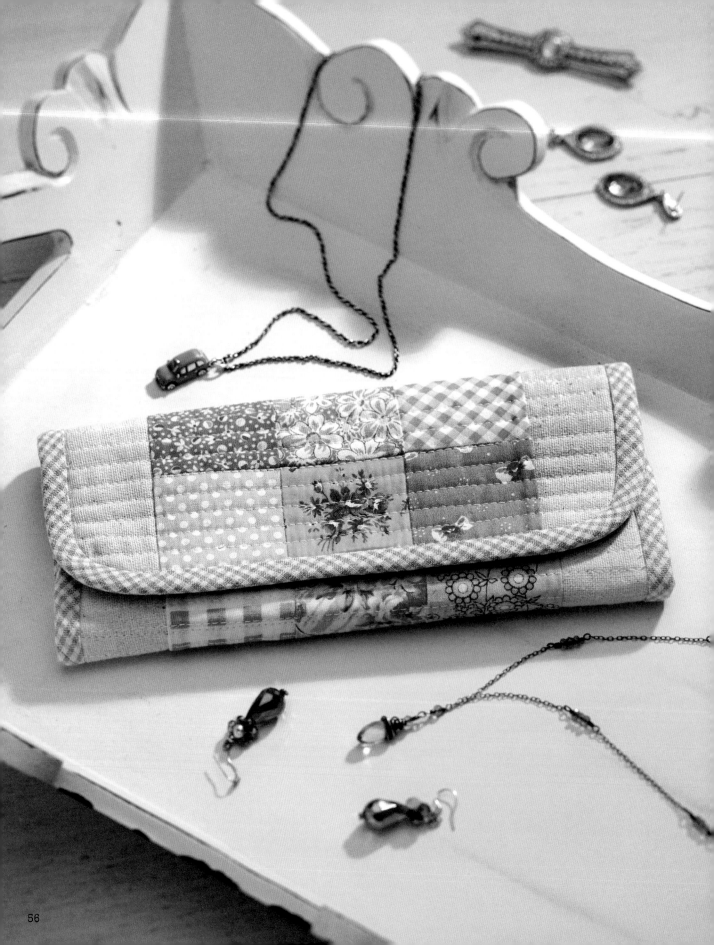

Pretty Patchwork Jewelry Wrap

DIFFICULTY
★★★

FINISHED SIZE
11" × 8¼" (27.9cm × 21cm)

Pretty patterned fabrics and gingham trim combine to make this cute jewelry wrap, which is perfect for storing special jewelry items or taking your favorite pieces with you on vacation. Featuring three internal zippered pockets and a snap closure, it's the perfect size to tuck into your suitcase or overnight bag.

WHAT IS OSNABURG?

Osnaburg is a coarse type of plain textile fabric, named for the city of Osnabrück, Germany. It was originally made from flax yarns, but it can be made from either flax, tow or jute yarns. It's softer than linen and does not wrinkle, which makes it perfect for wraps. If you're unable to find Osnaburg in your local fabric shop, try searching for it in online stores or use natural linen as a substitute.

MATERIALS

18 assorted scraps of fabric (a mix of florals, gingham and polka dots) measuring at least 2¼" (5.7cm) square.

Fat quarter of Osnaburg fabric in natural (or natural linen)

Fat quarter of cream floral print for lining and pockets

Fat eighth of pink cotton print for lining

Fat quarter of white quilt batting

Fat quarter of fusible fleece

Three 8" (20cm) zippers

2 yard (1.8m) package of ready-made ⅜" wide (1cm) bias tape

1 snap set, ½" (1.3cm) in diameter

TOOLS & SUPPLIES

Basic sewing tools (see Tools and Materials)

Snap press or snap pressing tool

¾" (19mm) bias tape maker

Note: All seam allowances are ¼" (6mm) unless otherwise noted.

CUTTING AND PREPARING FABRICS

From the following, cut

- Eighteen 2¼" (5.7cm) squares from the assorted prints for the wrap exterior
- Two 11" × 2¼" (27.9cm × 5.7cm) strips from the Osnaburg for the wrap exterior
- Two 1⅜" × 8¼" (3.5cm × 21cm) strips from the pink print for the strips that join the pockets

From the cream print, cut

- One 10" × 12" (25.4cm × 30.5cm) rectangle for the lining
- Two 5½" × 8¼" (14cm × 21cm) rectangles for the top and bottom pockets
- One 6" × 8¼" (15.2cm × 21cm) rectangle for the middle pocket
- One 10" × 12" (25.4cm × 30.5cm) rectangle from the quilt batting

From the fusible fleece, cut

- Two 2¾" × 8¼" (7cm × 21cm) rectangles for the top and bottom pockets
- One 3" × 8¼" (7.6cm × 21cm) rectangle for the middle pocket

ASSEMBLE THE EXTERIOR

1 Arrange the patchwork squares in 6 rows of 3. Begin stitching the first row of squares together by placing 2 squares together with the right sides facing and all edges matching. Pin, then stitch together along one side. Add another square in the same manner to create a row. Press all seam allowances to one side. Repeat for the remaining 5 rows, alternating the direction in which you press the seam allowances on each row.

2 With right sides facing and lining up all seams and edges, stitch the first 2 rows together. Press the seam allowances toward row 2. Repeat this step to stitch together rows 3, 4, 5 and 6.

3 Position the patchwork unit on a flat surface, right-side up. Lay the Osnaburg strips on top of each side, aligning and pinning the long edges. Stitch them together along the pinned edges. Press the seam allowance toward the patchwork (Figure 1).

4 Position the lining on a flat surface, wrong-side up. Layer the batting on top with the edges aligned. Center the patchwork panel on top, right-side up. Pin all the layers together with safety pins, approximately 2" (5.1cm) apart.

5 Starting in the center, quilt the patchwork unit in straight lines, approximately ⅜" (1cm) apart (Figure 2).

6 Trim the jewelry wrap exterior so it measures 11" × 8¼" (27.9cm × 21cm).

Figure 1

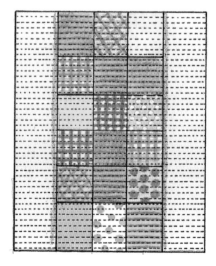

Figure 2

ASSEMBLE THE INTERIOR

7 Use the bias tape maker to make 2 strips measuring ¾" × 8¼" (1.9cm × 21cm). If you don't have a bias tape maker, press both long edges on the pink strips into the center.

8 For the top pocket, fold the pocket fabric in half lengthwise with wrong sides together and press. Open up the fabric and fuse the fusible fleece onto one side of the pocket fabric. Position the zipper so that it is on a flat surface in a horizontal position with the zipper pull located on the left side. Pin the pocket above the zipper so the folded edge of the pocket is approximately ¼" (6mm) above the zipper teeth. Stitch the pocket in place. Stitch the open end of the pocket together using a small zigzag stitch.

9 For the middle pocket, fold the pocket fabric in half lengthwise with wrong sides together and press. Open up the fabric and fuse the fusible fleece onto one side of the pocket fabric. Position the zipper so that it is on a flat surface in a horizontal position with the zipper pull located on the left side. Pin the pocket below the zipper so the folded edge of the pocket is approximately ¼" (6mm) below the zipper teeth. Stitch in place. Stitch the open end of the pocket together using a small zigzag stitch. Pin a pink bias strip above the zipper and stitch it in place.

10 To create the bottom pocket, repeat step 9 (Figure 3).

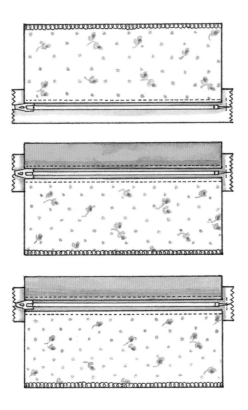

Figure 3

ASSEMBLE THE WRAP

11 Lay the exterior of the jewelry wrap on a flat surface so the lining is facing up. Position the bottom pocket so the bottom edge is aligned with the bottom edge of the wrap. Position the top pocket so the top edge is aligned with the top of the wrap. Position the middle pocket so it is centered. The pink strip above the middle pocket should cover the bottom edge of the top zipper. The pink edge of the bottom pocket should cover the bottom edge of the middle pocket. Pin the layers together. Topstitch around the 2 pink strips through all layers (Figure 4).

12 Baste around the outside of the jewelry wrap to hold all the layers together. Trim the ends of the zippers. Using a small drinking glass as a template, place the glass at each corner and trace around the curve with a water-soluble fabric pen to make a rounded edge. Trim along the marked line.

13 Unfold the ready-made bias binding. Pin the binding around the outside of the wrap exterior, over-lapping the ends by ¼" (6mm). Stitch the binding in place. Fold the binding over to the inside of the wrap and pin it in place. Hand-stitch the binding in position around the inside of the wrap (Figure 5).

14 To add the snap closure, open the top pocket. Make a small hole in the center of the pocket, approximately 1" (2.5cm) down from the top edge. Attach the snap cover and socket to the top pocket so the snap cover is hidden from view inside the pocket and the socket is visible at the top of the pocket. Open the bottom pocket and make a small hole in the center of the exterior/lining, about 2" (5.1cm) above the bottom edge of the wrap. Attach the snap and stud so the stud is facing out on the exterior side, and the snap is hidden from view inside the pocket.

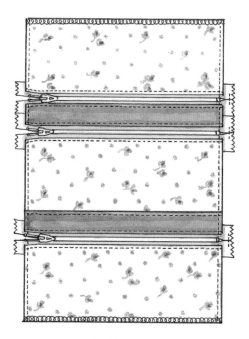

Figure 4

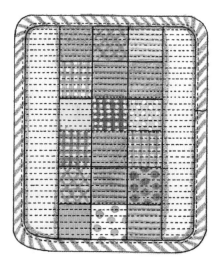

Figure 5

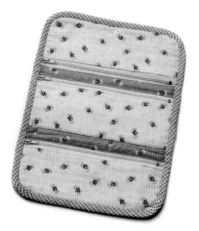

Dress Form Lavender Sachets

DIFFICULTY
★ ★ ☆

FINISHED SIZE
6½" × 4½" (16.5cm × 11.4cm), excluding the hanging loop

These French country-style lavender sachets will add a lovely scent to your clothing and help repel moths in your wardrobe or closet. They feature an appliquéd dress form and are decorated with lace, ribbons and trims. Combine ginghams, polka dots and small floral prints to make them suit your personal style or that of a friend.

MATERIALS

Fat eighth of gingham fabric for sachet front

Fat eighth of polka dot fabric for sachet back

Fat eighth of floral print for dress form appliqué

Fat eighth of white print for oval appliqué foundation

½ yard (45.7cm) of cotton lace or rickrack

¼ yard (22.9cm) of cotton tape for hanging loop

Scrap of brown print fabric for dress form appliqué

Scraps of ribbon or vintage French laundry tape

Fusible web

Polyester fiberfill

¼ cup of dried lavender buds

Scrap of muslin for the lavender

TOOLS & SUPPLIES

Basic sewing tools (see Tools and Materials)

Card stock for the template

Appliqué mat (optional)

Spray starch

Hera marker

TEMPLATES

Dressform Appliqué (on CD)

Note: All seam allowances are ¼" (6mm) unless otherwise indicated.

CUTTING AND PREPARING FABRICS

- From the gingham fabric, cut a 7" × 5" (17.8cm × 12.7cm) rectangle
- From the polka dot fabric, cut a 7" × 5" (17.8cm × 12.7cm) rectangle
- From the muslin, cut two 3" (7.6cm) squares

PREPARE APPLIQUÉ

1 Trace the oval template onto a piece of card stock and cut out the oval shape. Trace the oval onto the back of the white print fabric using a hera marker. Cut around the oval, adding a ¼" (6mm) seam allowance. Apply some spray starch to the seam allowance of the fabric oval. Position the fabric oval with the wrong side facing up. Place the oval template made from the card onto the fabric and center it. Using your iron, gently press the seam allowance over the card, so when the oval is turned over the right way, the seam allowance has been pressed under.

2 Using the dress form template, trace the dress form and the wooden stand onto the back of the fusible web. Cut around the shapes leaving at least ¼" (6mm) clearance. Press the dress form onto the back of the floral print. Cut out the dress form shape. Press the wooden stand onto the back of the brown print fabric. Cut out the base and the top of the stand. Peel off the paper backing and position the dress form and wooden stand on the white oval fabric (refer to the photograph for placement). Press in place.

3 Using coordinated thread, stitch around the shapes. Stay close to the edge using a stitch length of 2.

4 If you desire, add a small decoration such as a vintage French laundry tape monogram or flag to the lower right side of the oval and stitch it in place.

Figure 1

ASSEMBLE SACHET

5 Center the appliquéd dress form on the front of the gingham fabric. Pin in place. Pin the lace trim or rickrack under the edge of the oval. Hand-stitch the oval and trim to the gingham (Figure 1).

6 To make a small tag, cut a piece of ribbon or tape measuring 2" (5.1cm). Fold the ribbon in half. Baste it in place approximately 1" (2.5cm) above the bottom right-hand corner.

7 To make the hanging loop, cut a piece of ribbon or tape measuring 6" (15.2cm) in length. Center the ends of the ribbon on the top of the sachet and baste them in place.

8 Layer the front and back of the sachet with the right sides facing. Stitch around the outside of the sachet, leaving a 2" (5.1cm) gap along the bottom edge for stuffing. Clip the corners and turn the sachet right-side out. Press.

9 Stitch the 2 squares of muslin together leaving a 1½" (3.8cm) gap in one side for turning. Turn the square right-side out. Fill it with dried lavender buds and stitch the opening closed.

10 Gently fill the sachet with fiberfill. Insert the lavender bag. Hand-stitch the opening closed.

MONOGRAMMED TAPE

French haberdashers used to sell boxes of monogrammed tape, traditionally in red and white. The tape was used to identify clothing and linens that were sent out to laundries.

CHAPTER 3

Kitchen

Our kitchen is the heart of our home and one of my favorite places to spend time. I love to bake and prepare meals for family and friends. Sewing practical items for the kitchen adds a welcoming touch. Make a *Gorgeous Gingham Pot Holder*, a *Handy Eco Shopper*, a stylish *Denim Café Apron* or the whimsical *Love-to-Bake Wall Art* to add some warmth to your kitchen. These projects make great hostess or housewarming gifts.

Gorgeous Gingham Pot Holder

DIFFICULTY
★ ★ ☆

FINISHED SIZE
7½" × 9½" (19.1cm × 24.1cm)

Floral, gingham and polka dots are combined in this lovely pot holder that features a panel of chicken scratch embroidery on the pocket. This fun project lets you practice your chicken scratch embroidery and adds some retro charm to your kitchen. If you're making this as a gift for a baker, you might want to include some cookie cutters or other baking tools.

MATERIALS

Fat eighth of cotton gingham (medium-size gingham with the checks spaced ¼" [6mm] apart) for chicken scratch panel

Fat quarter of floral print for pot holder front and back

Fat eighth of plain homespun for pocket lining

Fat quarter of polka-dot cotton print for ruffle

Fat quarter of small floral print for bias binding

Fat quarter of fusible fleece

Fat quarter of quilt batting

Fat quarter of insulated batting (such as Insul-Brite)

1 skein of white perle 5 thread

1 skein of red perle 5 thread

¼ yard (22.9cm) of ½" (1.3cm) wide twill tape for hanging loop

TOOLS & SUPPLIES

Basic sewing tools (see Tools and Materials)

¾" (19mm) bias tape maker

1" (2.5cm) wide masking tape

Safety pins

Embroidery needle

TEMPLATES

Stitching Graph (on CD)

Note: Seam allowances are ¼" (6mm) wide unless otherwise indicated.

CUTTING AND PREPARING FABRICS

From the following, cut

- One 8" (20.3cm) square from the gingham print
- Two 8" × 10" (20.3cm × 25.4cm) rectangles from the floral print
- One 8" (20.3cm) square from the homespun
- One 2¼" × 15" (5.7cm × 38.1cm) strip from the polka-dot fabric
- One 8" (20.3cm) square from the fusible fleece
- One 8" × 10" (20.3cm × 25.4cm) rectangle from the insulated batting
- One 6" (15.2cm) length of twill tape

From the quilt batting, cut

- One 8" (20.3cm) square
- One 8" × 10" (20.3cm × 25.4cm) rectangle

From the small floral print, cut

- Two 2¼" × 20" (5.7cm × 50.8cm) bias strips
- One 1⅜" × 8" (3.5cm × 20.3cm) bias strip

CREATE CHICKEN SCRATCH EMBROIDERY PANEL

1 Fuse the fusible fleece to the back of the gingham fabric. Refer to the stitching graph and stitch a combination of cross-stitch, woven squares (2 loops), and woven circles (4 loops). Center the design on the gingham square (refer to Chicken Scratch in the Embroidery Techniques section).

2 Lightly press the chicken scratch panel from the back of the fabric. Trim the gingham to 7½" (19.1cm) square, with the embroidery centered on the panel.

ASSEMBLE THE EMBROIDERED POCKET

3 Position the square of homespun on top of the square of quilt batting with all the edges aligned. Baste the 2 layers together with safety pins. Using the masking tape, mark a straight line from the top left-hand corner to the bottom right-hand corner. Quilt the layers together on a 45° angle. Move the masking tape and continue quilting straight lines 1" (2.5cm) apart on a 45° angle (Figure 1). Position the masking tape from the top right-hand corner to the bottom left-hand corner and position the quilt lines in the opposite direction so the pocket lining is quilted in a crosshatch design. Press the pocket lining and trim it so that it measures 7½" (19.1cm) square.

4 Press the polka-dot fabric strip in half lengthwise with wrong sides facing. Stitch along the open edge, ⅛" (3mm) from the edge using a stitch length of 4. Pull on the threads to gather the ruffle so it's 7½" (19.1cm) in length. Pin the ruffle to the top edge of the chicken scratch front pocket. Baste in place (Figure 2).

5 Position the embroidered panel on top of the quilted homespun with all the edges aligned. Baste around the outside of the pocket, using a scant seam allowance. Take the 1⅜" × 8" (3.5cm × 20.3cm) bias strip and feed it through the bias tape maker to create a bias strip. Open out the bias tape and pin it along the top edge of the pocket with right sides facing. Stitch the tape in place. Fold the tape over the top of the pocket to enclose the raw edge. Pin the tape to the back of the pocket and hand-stitch in place to secure. Trim the ends of the bias binding.

ASSEMBLE THE POT HOLDER

6 Position the rectangle of insulated batting on top of the rectangle of quilt batting with the shiny side facing up (be sure to note which side is the shiny side, as it will need to be closest to the heat source when the potholder is used). Sandwich the 2 layers of batting between the 2 rectangles of floral print with the print facing out. Baste the 4 layers together with safety pins, and then quilt using a 45° angle crosshatch design (as you did in step 3), spaced 1" (2.5cm) apart. Lightly press using an iron. Trim the back of the pot holder to 7½" × 9½" (19.1cm × 24.1cm).

7 Position the pocket on top of the pot holder so the bottom edges are aligned. Baste the bottom and sides in place using a scant seam allowance. Using a small drinking glass as a template, place the glass at each corner and trace around the curve with a water-soluble fabric pen to make a rounded edge. Trim to shape. Stitch around the outside of the pot holder using a zigzag stitch to flatten the edges.

8 Fold the twill tape in half. Pin the ends of the twill tape to the back of the pot holder on the top right-hand corner so the edges of the tape are aligned with the edge of the pot holder. Stitch the ends of the tape to secure.

9 Stitch the 2 bias strips together at 45°. Press the seam open. Press the strip in half lengthwise. With the front of the pot holder facing, pin the bias strip around the outside of the pot holder so that the edge of the bias strip is aligned with the edge of the pot holder. Ease the bias strip around the rounded corners. Stitch around the outside of the pot holder to secure the bias binding. Fold the binding over to the back of the pot holder and pin in place. Hand-stitch the binding to the back of the pot holder to secure it.

CHICKEN SCRATCH

Chicken scratch embroidery (also known as Broderie Suisse, Australian Cross Stitch, and Depression Lace) is an easy style of embroidery that is worked on gingham fabric to create a lacy effect.

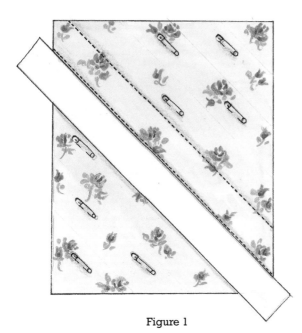

Figure 1

Figure 2

Handy Eco Shopper

DIFFICULTY
★ ☆ ☆

FINISHED SIZE
16" × 19½" (40.6cm × 49.5cm) (bag)
6¼" × 4" (15.9cm × 10.2cm) (pouch)

The environmentally conscious shopper will appreciate this handy eco-bag that was inspired by the plastic grocery sack. When not in use, it folds up to fit inside a small pouch that's easily stowed in your handbag or travel bag. The bag is unlined so it's light for travelers, and it features French seams for added strength and a neat finish.

MATERIALS
½ yard (45.7cm) floral print for bag and pouch

½ yard (45.7cm) polka dot fabric for bag and pouch

7" (17.8cm) ribbon or trim for pouch

TOOLS & SUPPLIES
Basic sewing tools (see Tools and Materials)

Hem guide tool

TEMPLATES
Bag Upper (on CD)

Note: All seam allowances are ¼" (6mm) unless otherwise indicated.

CUTTING AND PREPARING FABRICS

From the floral print fabric, cut

- 2 bag shapes using the template provided (bag upper). Position the template on a fold of fabric as indicated.
- One 6¾" × 4½" (17.1cm × 11.4cm) rectangle (pouch)

From the polka-dot fabric, cut

- Two 17" × 7½" (43.2cm × 44.4cm) rectangles (bag lower)
- One 6¾" (17.1cm) square (pouch)

ASSEMBLE THE BAG

1 Position one floral panel (bag upper) and a polka-dot panel (bag lower) with the wrong sides together, aligning the 17" (43.2cm) edges at the bottom of the floral panel. Pin and sew together along the pinned edge so the exposed seam is on the front of the bag. Trim the seam allowance to ⅛" (3mm). Open the seam and press the seam allowance toward the polka-dot fabric. Press on the wrong side to ensure the seam is flat. Fold the fabric on the seam with right sides together. Press the seam flat so the stitching is on the

edge of the fold. Pin along the pressed edges and stitch along the edge with a ¼" (6mm) seam. The raw edge will now be enclosed neatly within the seam allowance. Topstitch ⅛" (3mm) below the seam. Repeat with the remaining bag pieces to create both sides of the bag.

2 Using a hem guide, fold under ¼" (6mm) along the top opening of the bag. Finger press. Turn under another ¼" (6mm) and pin the edge in position. Carefully stitch around the top opening of the bag from one handle to the other. Press. Fold under ¼" (6mm) along the outside edge of both handles. Finger press. Turn under a further ¼" (6mm). Pin in place and then stitch. Repeat for the other bag panel (Figure 1).

3 Place the bag front on top of the bag back with the wrong sides facing and all edges aligned. Pin the side seams. Stitch the side seams. Trim the seam allowance to ⅛" (3mm). Turn the bag wrong-side out. Press the side seams. Pin along the pressed edge and stitch with a ¼" (6mm) seam. Press. Turn the bag right-side out.

4 Along the bottom edge of the bag, use pins to mark 2¼" (5.7cm) from the side seams on both the front and back of the bag. Also mark 4½" (11.4cm) from the side seams on the front and back of the bag.

5 Fold the side seams inward so the side seam is aligned with the pins at the 4½" (11.4cm) mark. Stitch in place along the bottom edge (Figure 2). Trim the seam allowance to ⅛" (3mm). Turn the bag inside out. Press the bag. Stitch along the bottom edge of the bag (Figure 3).

Figure 1

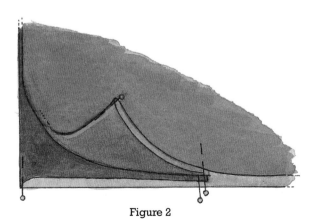

Figure 2

6 Turn the bag right-side out. Pin the bag handles together at the top of the bag. Stitch in place. Trim the seam allowance to ⅛" (3mm). Turn the bag inside out. Press the handles at the join. Stitch along the pressed seam line.

ASSEMBLE THE POUCH

7 Along the top of the polka-dot rectangle, turn under ¼" (6mm) of fabric along the top edge. Press. Turn under an additional ¼" (6mm). Pin the fabric in place and stitch to secure the hem. On the right side, pin the ribbon ⅛" (3mm) from the hemmed edge and stitch in place.

8 Along the top edge of the floral rectangle, turn under ¼" (6mm) and press. Turn under another ¼" (6mm) and stitch in place.

9 Place the floral rectangle on top of the polka-dot rectangle with right sides together and the bottom edges (unhemmed edges) aligned. Stitch along the bottom edge. Serge the raw edge.

10 Lay the pouch fabric so the right side is facing up. Fold down the top of the pouch so the side of the pouch measures 4" (10.2cm) from the bottom seam to the top of the fold (Figure 4). Baste in place along the sides. Fold the floral fabric at the bottom seam and position the floral fabric so it's positioned on top of the polka-dot fabric (Figure 5). Stitch the side seams in place. Serge the raw edges. Clip the corners and turn the pouch right-side out.

Figure 3

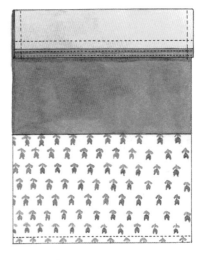

Figure 4

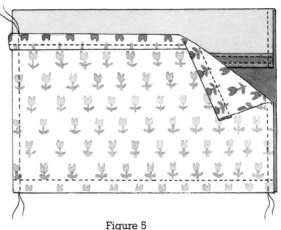

Figure 5

TIP

To fit the eco-bag into the pouch, fold it into thirds, and then into thirds again so it measures approximately 6" × 4" (15.2cm × 10.2cm).

Denim Café Apron

DIFFICULTY
★★☆

FINISHED SIZE
26" × 15" (66cm × 38.1cm),
with 34" (86.4cm) straps

This stylish and practical café apron is made from durable denim and features a patchwork pocket and sashiko stitching detail. The patchwork is the perfect way to showcase handprinted organic fabrics.

MATERIALS

½ yard (45.7cm) of denim

20 assorted scraps of screen-printed fabric, measuring at least 3" × 2½" (7.6cm × 6.4cm) each

½ yard (45.7cm) of piping

2 yards (1.8m) of 1¼" (3.2cm) wide twill tape

Fat quarter of cotton fabric for pocket lining

Ribbon for embellishment (optional)

1 skein of sashiko thread

TOOLS & SUPPLIES

Basic sewing tools (refer to Tools and Materials)

Sashiko needle

Tailor's chalk

Note: Seam allowances are ¼" (6mm) wide unless otherwise indicated.

CUTTING AND PREPARING FABRICS

From the following, cut

- One 28" × 18" (71.1cm × 45.7cm) rectangle from the denim fabric
- One 12½" × 6½" (31.8cm × 16.5cm) rectangle from the cotton fabric for the pocket lining

From the screen-printed scraps, cut

- Eighteen 2½" (6.4cm) squares for the patchwork pocket
- Two 3" × 1¾" (7.6cm × 4.4cm) rectangles for the straps

PREPARE THE APRON

1 Fold and press under ½" (1.3cm) along the bottom edge of the denim rectangle. Fold and press a further ½" (1.3cm) along the folded edge. Stitch close to the edge of the hem to secure.

2 Draw a horizontal line using tailor's chalk that is ¾" (1.9cm) above the bottom of the apron. Draw a second line that is ⅞" (2.2cm) above the bottom of the apron. Draw a third line that is 1" (2.5cm) above the bottom of the apron.

3 Using the sashiko thread, stitch a sashiko-style running stitch along each of the 3 lines.

4 Fold and press under ½" (1.3cm) along one side edge of the apron. Fold in an additional ½" (1.3cm) and press. Topstitch close to the edge. Repeat for the remaining side.

PREPARE THE PATCHWORK POCKET

5 Arrange the 18 patchwork squares into 3 rows of 6 patches. Begin stitching the first row of squares together by placing 2 squares with right sides together, matching up all edges. Pin them together and stitch along one edge. Add another square in the same manner. Continue adding the remainder of the squares in row 1. Press all the seam allowances to one side. Repeat this process for row 2, pressing the seam allowances in the opposite direction. Repeat for the third row.

6 Stitch the first 2 rows together, placing them right-sides together and lining up all the seams and edges. Pin them together and stitch. Repeat the process to stitch row 2 to row 3. You now have a patchwork panel that measures 12½" × 6½" (31.8cm × 16.5cm).

7 Pin the piping along the top of the pocket lining so the raw edge of the piping and the top edge of the pocket lining are aligned. Stitch together close to the piping with a basting stitch. Position the pocket lining on top of the patchwork panel so the right edges are facing and all edges are aligned. Pin in place and stitch around the perimeter of the lining, leaving a 4" (10.2cm) gap along the bottom edge of the pocket for turning. Clip corners, and turn right-side out through the gap in the lining. Press the pocket. Topstitch ¼" (6mm) above the seam that joins row 1 to row 2 through all layers. Topstitch ¼" (6mm) above the seam that joins row 2 to row 3 (Figure 1).

8 Pin the pocket to the apron so it's centered and positioned 4" (10.2cm) above the bottom edge. If desired, insert a 2" (5.1cm) piece of folded ribbon under the bottom right-hand side of the pocket, tucking its raw edges under the pocket. Topstitch the pocket to the apron along the sides and bottom edge, enclosing the gap in the lining and attaching the ribbon accent as you sew.

9 To create a divided pocket, stitch a line from the top of the pocket down to the bottom of the pocket, ¼" (6mm) to the left of the seam that joins column 4 to column 5.

MAKE THE APRON

10 Fold down ½" (1.3cm) along the top edge of the apron and press. Fold down another 1¼" (3.2cm) and press. Cut the twill tape into 2 equal pieces. Place one short raw edge of twill tape inside the waistband fold with roughly 1" (2.5cm) of the tape inside the fold and pin it in place. Repeat for the other strap. Topstitch all edges of the fold along the top of the apron.

11 Try on the apron and adjust the length of the straps, if necessary. To make the fabric tabs to place over the ends of the apron straps, take a fabric rectangle that measures 3" × 1¾" (7.6cm × 4.4cm). Fold under ¼" (6mm) on one long side and fold the unit in half with right sides facing so you have a piece measuring 1¾" × 1¼" (4.4cm × 3.2cm). Stitch the top and unfolded side seams of the unit. Clip the corners and turn the unit right-side out. Slip the unit over the raw edge of the herringbone tape (using a bamboo skewer or an awl to push the end of the tape down inside the fabric unit). Hand-stitch the opening of the fabric cover to the tape (Figure 2). Make a second unit with the remaining piece of fabric to cover the end of the remaining apron strap.

TIP

Look for some handprinted fabric scraps from independent screen-print designers on Etsy or experiment with printing your own.

Figure 1

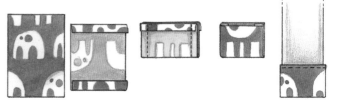

Figure 2

Love-to-Bake Wall Art

DIFFICULTY
★ ☆ ☆

FINISHED SIZE
10" (25.4cm) diameter

Baking is one of my favorite hobbies (after sewing of course!). This hoop art project features an appliquéd stand mixer and is the perfect gift for a baking lover to hang in the kitchen.

MATERIALS

Fat quarter of white background fabric for appliqué foundation

Fabric scraps for the appliqué including aqua polka dot (7" [17.8cm] square), gray print (5" × 4" [12.7cm × 10.2cm]), red print (2" [5.1cm] square), text print (4" × 1½" [10.2cm × 3.8cm])

Fusible double-sided web

10" (25.4cm) embroidery hoop

1 skein of white perle 5 thread

TOOLS & SUPPLIES

Basic sewing tools (see Tools and Materials)

1 sheet of white cardstock (10" [25.4cm] square)

Appliqué mat (optional)

Compass

TEMPLATES

Mixer Appliqué (on CD)

CUTTING AND PREPARING FABRICS

- Cut a 14" (35.6cm) square using the white background fabric
- With a compass, draw a circle with a 10" (25.4cm) diameter onto white cardstock and cut it out.

PREPARE AND STITCH APPLIQUÉ

1 Trace all the pieces for the mixer (in reverse) onto the paper back of the fusible web. You will have a mixer stand, a bowl, a heart, two labels and a small button. Cut these shapes out, leaving approximately ¼" (6mm) around each shape.

2 Fuse the shapes onto the back of the fabric following manufacturer's directions. Refer to the photograph to see the fabrics used for each piece.

3 Cut around the shapes on the fabric. Peel off the paper backing. Referring to the photograph, center the mixer and its components on the background square of fabric. Fuse the shapes to the background with the iron.

4 Stitch around each component of the mixer using black thread in your sewing machine. Stitch around each component 3 times. Vary the line of stitching so it gives the outline a sketchy appearance. Press the appliqué.

MULTIPLE USES

Appliqué the stand mixer onto a plain tea towel or turn the appliqué into a trivet or pot holder.

ASSEMBLE THE WALL ART

5 Cut the background square into a 14" (35.6cm) circle. Position the completed appliqué in the wooden hoop so it's centered. Tighten the hoop so that the fabric is taut.

6 Position the white cardstock in the back of the hoop to cover the back of the stitching.

7 Fold under ⅜" (1cm) around the raw edge of the fabric. Using the perle thread, run a gathering stitch around the outside of the circle next to the fold in the fabric. Pull the ends of the embroidery thread so the fabric is gathered and tie off the ends of the thread.

Craft Room

If you love to sew, nothing is better than making practical little projects that you can use in your sewing room or craft space. Small projects are a great way to try out and practice new techniques before committing time and energy to larger projects such as quilts. In this chapter, you'll find a patchwork *Sewing Portfolio* to store your embroidery or paper piecing projects, a *Zakka Dilly Bag* for crochet projects, *Fabric Gift Baskets* to organize your buttons and trims, and *Cathedral Window Pincushions*. These projects are perfect for organizing your sewing supplies and for crafting on the go. Make a few extras to give as gifts to your crafty friends and sewing swap partners.

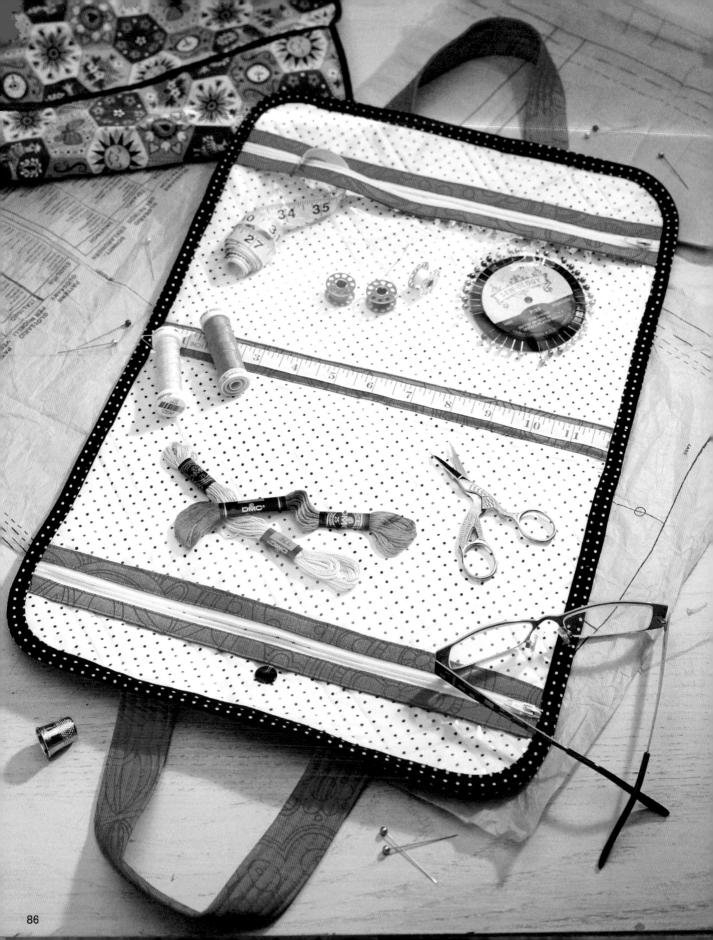

Sewing Portfolio

DIFFICULTY
★ ★ ★

FINISHED SIZE
12½" × 18½" (31.8cm × 47cm), excluding the handles

This handy sewing portfolio is perfect for storing hand sewing and embroidery projects when you're on the go. Featuring two large clear-plastic internal pockets and a sewn-in tape measure, it is constructed from hourglass blocks in shades of pink, white and black.

MATERIALS

12 assorted pink fabric scraps, measuring at least 4½" × 4½" (11.4cm × 11.4cm) for patchwork

12 assorted low-volume fabric scraps in white, black, gray or off-white, measuring at least 4½" (11.4cm) square for patchwork

Fat quarter of white cotton print for lining

Fat quarter of pink print for handles and closure tab

Fat quarter of batting

Plastic tape measure

½ yard (45.7cm) of clear tablecloth plastic

1 package of ready-made ⅜" (1cm) wide double-fold bias tape

1 snap closure

Two 12" (30.5cm) zippers

Scrap of fusible interfacing

TOOLS & SUPPLIES

Basic sewing tools (see Tools and Materials)

Snap setting tool or snap press

Sewing stiletto or awl

1" (2.5cm) bias tape maker

Safety pins

TEMPLATE

Tab (on CD)

Note: All seam allowances are ¼" (6mm) unless otherwise indicated.

CUTTING AND PREPARING FABRICS

From the pink fabrics, cut twelve 4½" (11.4cm) squares.

From the low-volume prints, cut twelve 4½" (11.4cm) squares.

From the pink print, cut

- Two 12½" × 5" (31.8cm × 12.7cm) strips for the handles
- 2 tab shapes from the Tab template
- Five 12½" × 1⅞" (31.8cm × 4.8cm) strips

From the plastic, cut

- One 12½" × 13½" (31.8cm × 34.3cm) rectangle
- Two 12½" × 2½" (31.8cm × 6.4cm) strips

From the tape measure, remove the metal cover on the ends and cut a length from 0 to 12".

From the fusible fleece, and using the Tab template, cut 2 tab shapes. Press the interfacing onto the wrong side of both pink tab pieces.

From the white cotton lining fabric, cut a 19" × 13" (48.3cm × 33cm) rectangle.

From the batting, cut

- One 19" × 13" (48.3cm × 33cm) rectangle
- Two 12½" × 1¼" (31.8cm × 3.2cm) strips

HOURGLASS BLOCKS

The hourglass block is a traditional quilt block that has been given a modern look in this scrappy project. By choosing a color scheme, you can give your scraps a more cohesive look.

PATCHWORK PANEL

1 To make the hourglass blocks, layer a pink square on top of a low-volume square with right sides facing and all the edges aligned. Using a water-soluble fabric pen, mark a diagonal line from the top left-hand corner down to the bottom right-hand corner. Pin the square together. With a ¼" (6mm) presser foot, stitch on either side of the marked line from edge to edge. Using a rotary cutter, cut on the marked diagonal line. Open the square and press the seam toward the pink fabric. Repeat until all 12 sets of squares have been sewn. You should now have squares that are half pink and half low volume.

2 Layer 2 of the squares together with right sides facing and all the edges aligned. The pink side of one square should be sitting above the low-volume side of the corresponding square with seams nested together. Mark a diagonal line from one corner to the other, perpendicular to the seam. Stitch ¼" (6mm) on each side of the marked line. Using a rotary cutter, cut the marked diagonal line. Open the square and press the seam allowance to one side (Figure 1). Repeat until you have 24 hourglass blocks.

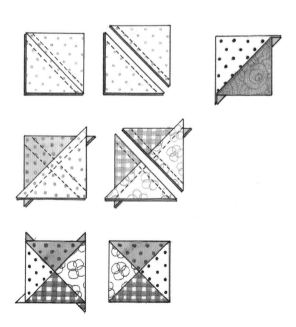

Figure 1

3 Trim the hourglass blocks to 3½" (8.9cm) square. To trim them to size, match the 45° line on your ruler with the diagonal seam line. Match the midpoint of 1¾" (4.4cm) with the intersection of the center seams and trim to size (Figure 1).

4 Arrange the hourglass blocks so you have 6 rows of 4 blocks. Arrange the blocks so the direction of the pink triangles alternates between adjacent blocks. Take the first 2 blocks of the first row and layer them together with right sides facing so all edges are aligned. Pin the blocks along the right side. Stitch the blocks together and press the seam allowance open. Continue adding blocks to the row and sewing them together until you have 6 rows of 4 blocks.

5 Layer the first 2 rows so the right sides are facing, and all edges and seams are aligned. Pin together, and then stitch using ¼" (6mm) seam allowance. Press the seam open. Continue adding rows in this way until all the rows are added and you have an hourglass panel that measures 12½" × 18½" (31.8cm × 47cm).

6 Place the lining piece face down on a flat surface. Add the batting and ensure that all edges are aligned. Add the patchwork panel with the right-side up. Pin the 3 layers together with safety pins. Machine quilt ¼" (6mm) from each diagonal seam or as desired. Trim the patchwork panel to 12½" × 18½" (31.8cm × 47cm) (Figure 2).

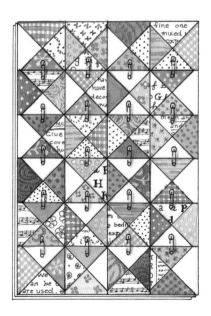

Figure 2

PREPARE THE HANDLES AND THE CLOSURE TAB

7 Fold the pink 12½" × 5" (31.8cm × 12.7cm) strip in half lengthwise with wrong sides together and press. Open up the strip and press the long edges into the center fold. Fold the strip in half so you now have a strip that measures 1¼" × 12½" (3.2cm × 31.8cm). Open up the fabric and place a strip of batting inside so the long edge of the batting is aligned with the center fold of the fabric strip. Refold the fabric on the fold lines. Quilt the handle lengthwise in straight lines ¼" (6mm) apart, starting ⅛" (3mm) from the edge. Repeat for the other handle.

8 Position the handle so the outside edge of the handle is in line with the seam that runs between blocks 1 and 2 on one of the short edges of the patchwork panel. Pin the handle in place. Position the other end of the handle so that the outside edge is in line with the seam that joins blocks 3 and 4. Baste both ends of the handle in place, using a scant seam allowance. Repeat for the other handle on the other short edge. (See photograph for placement.)

9 Place the 2 interfaced tab shapes with right sides together and all edges aligned. Stitch around the edge from one side to the other, leaving the short edge open. Clip the curves. Turn the tab right-side out, using a chopstick for turning. Press the tab. Topstitch around the outside using a ⅛" (3mm) seam allowance.

10 Position the tab so it's centered between the handle on one of the short sides. This will become the back of the portfolio. Pin the tab in place and baste to the patchwork panel with a scant seam allowance (Figure 3).

PREPARE THE INSIDE OF THE PORTFOLIO

11 Take the 5 pink strips measuring 12½" × 1⅞" (31.8cm × 4.8cm) and feed them, one at a time, through the bias tape maker, until you have 5 strips measuring 12½" × 1" (31.8cm × 2.5cm). Fold 4 of these strips in half lengthwise to make double-fold strips, then press. They will now measure 12½" × ½" (31.8cm × 1.3cm).

12 Position the length of tape measure in the middle of the single-fold bias strip (12½" × 1" [31.8cm × 2.5cm] strip) so it's centered. Pin to hold it in position. Stitch around the tape measure using a scant ⅛" (3mm) seam allowance.

13 Take the large rectangle of plastic and place a double-fold bias strip along one of the short edges. Pin the bias strip in place. Stitch along the inside edge of the bias strip, ⅛" (3mm) from the inside edge. Add another bias strip to the opposite side of the large plastic panel using the same method. Stitch a bias strip to one long edge of each of the 2 plastic strips using the same method.

14 Lay one of the bound edges of the large plastic rectangle over one of the zippers, with the zipper pull on the left-hand side (Figure 4). Stitch the zipper in place using a zipper foot on the sewing machine. Position the second zipper on the opposite side with the zipper pull (also on the left-hand side) and stitch it in place.

15 Add the plastic strips to the outside edges of the 2 zippers so that the bound edge is stitched on top of the zipper using the same method used in step 14. Trim the plastic panel so that it measures 12½" × 18½" (31.8cm × 47cm) (Figure 5).

16 Lay the plastic sheet on top of the sewing portfolio lining, with all the edges aligned, and baste around the outside of the portfolio using a scant seam allowance.

Figure 3

Make sure the handles and tab are folded in toward the portfolio. Use a medium drinking glass approximately 3" (7.6cm) in diameter as a template, placing it at each corner and drawing around the curve with a water-soluble fabric pen to make a rounded corner. Cut along the rounded line (Figure 6).

17 Position the tape measure strip so that the bottom edge of the strip is aligned with the middle of the portfolio. Pin the strip in place and then stitch around the outside of the strip, through all the layers. This will divide the plastic into 2 pockets.

18 Unfold the bias tape. Fold the short edge of the bias tape under ½" (1.3cm) and pin it around the outside edge (perimeter) of the sewing portfolio. Sew the bias tape in place. Fold the bias tape over the exposed edge and pin it in place. Stitch around the edge of the portfolio though all layers to secure the bias tape, being careful to avoid the ends of the zipper.

19 Using a snap press or snap-setting tool, attach the snap to the tab where it's marked on the template. Position the corresponding snap part on the outside of the portfolio, referring to the photograph for placement.

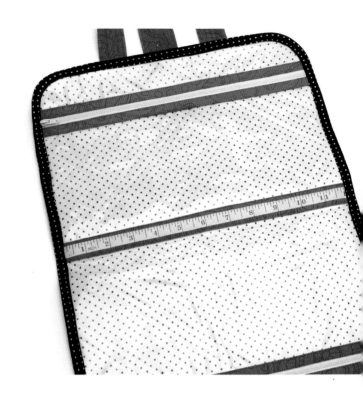

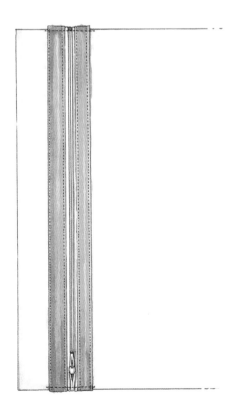

Figure 4

Figure 5

Figure 6

Fabric Gift Baskets

DIFFICULTY
★ ★ ☆

FINISHED SIZE
3" (7.6cm) in height, with a diameter of 4¼" (10.8cm)

These adorable fabric baskets are quick to sew, not to mention perfect for storing and organizing so many items. Made from home-décor-weight fabric and lined with a novelty print quilting cotton, they feature a fabric and felt label. Fill them with small items such as craft supplies, baby items or pantry items. Your friends will love receiving a gift in a fabric basket—it's like receiving two gifts in one!

MATERIALS (makes 1 basket)

Fat eighth of home-décor-weight cotton fabric (medium to heavyweight)

Fat eighth of quilting cotton

Fusible fleece

Small piece of coordinating quilting cotton

Fusible web

Small piece of felt

TOOLS & SUPPLIES

Basic sewing tools (see Tools and Materials)

Appliqué mat

Compass or fabric die-cutting machine with a 2" (5.1cm) circle die

TEMPLATE

Basket Base (on CD)

Note: All seam allowances are ¼" (6mm) unless indicated otherwise.

CUTTING AND PREPARING FABRICS

From the home-décor-weight fabric (blue polka dot), cut

- One 3" × 15" (7.6cm × 38.1cm) rectangle
- 1 circular base, using the Basket Base template

From the quilting cotton (for milk labels), cut

- One 3½" × 15" (8.9cm × 38.1cm) rectangle
- 1 circular base, using the Basket Base template

From the coordinating cotton, cut

- One 1" × 15" (2.5cm × 38.1cm) strip

From the fusible fleece, cut

- One 3½" × 15" (8.9cm × 38.1cm) rectangle
- 1 circular base, using the Basket Base template

PREPARE FABRIC LABEL

1 Select a small image on your lining fabric to use as the circular label (approximately 1½" [3.8cm] in diameter). Cut a small piece of fusible web that's slightly larger than the image and iron it onto the wrong side of the fabric, following the manufacturer's directions. Use your appliqué mat to protect your iron and ironing board. Cut around the image so you have a circular label approximately 1½" (3.8cm) in diameter.

2 Use a compass to draw a circle that is 2" (5.1cm) in diameter onto a piece of felt and cut it out. (Alternatively, use your die-cutting machine and a 2" (5.1cm) circle die to cut a felt circle that is 2" (5.1cm) in diameter).

3 Peel the backing paper from your fabric image, position it in the center of your felt circle and fuse it into position using your iron. Stitch around the outside of your fabric circle, through the felt, using a small stitch length. Cut a piece of fusible web that is 2" (5.1cm) in diameter. Fuse it onto the back of the felt circle.

ASSEMBLE THE BASKET

4 With right sides together and edges aligned, stitch along the top edge of the home-décor-fabric rectangle

and the fabric strip. Press the seam open. Fuse the rectangle of fusible fleece to the wrong side of the fabric. Topstitch next to the seam, on the home décor fabric.

5 Position the fabric label in the center of the home décor fabric, so it's approximately ¼" (6mm) below the seam. Fuse the label in place. Stitch around the outside of the label using a small stitch length (Figure 1).

6 Stitch the 2 short edges together, with right sides facing, to form the sides of the basket. On the bottom edge of this tube, mark 4 equal sections 3⅝" (9.2cm) apart using a water-soluble fabric pen.

Figure 1

7 Fuse the batting to the circular base of the basket. Fold the circular base into quarters and mark each quarter with the water-soluble fabric pen.

8 With right sides together, match the marks on the circle with the marks on the tube edge. Align the raw edges and pin it in place. Continue pinning around the bottom edge of the circle base. Stitch the circular base to the sides of the basket. Stitch slowly and carefully. It's easier to sew a circular shape to a straight edge (Figure 2).

ASSEMBLE THE LINING

9 With right sides together, sew the short edges of the lining panel together, leaving a 2¼" (5.7cm) gap in the middle of the seam. On the bottom of the lining tube, mark 4 equal sections 3⅝" (9.2cm) apart, as you did for the basket exterior. Fold the circular base of the lining into quarters and mark each quarter with a water-soluble fabric pen.

10 Pin the circular base of the lining to the lining sides as you did for the exterior of the basket. Stitch in place.

FINISH THE BASKET

11 Place the outer basket inside the lining so the right sides are facing. Pin them together at the top edge, ensuring the back seam is aligned. Stitch around the top of the basket (Figure 3).

12 Turn the basket right-side out through the gap in the lining. It's a tight fit, so carefully ease a little out at a time. Hand-stitch the gap in the lining closed using a ladder stitch. Topstitch around the top opening of the basket. Press the basket, using some spray starch to smooth the lining.

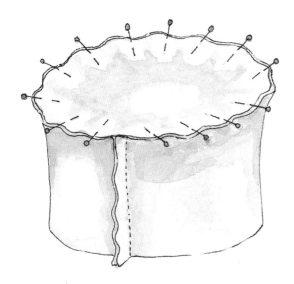

Figure 2

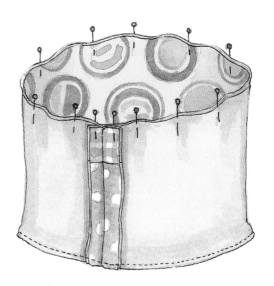

Figure 3

Zakka Dilly Bag

DIFFICULTY
★ ★ ☆

FINISHED SIZE
9¾" (24.8cm) in height with a 6" (15.2cm)
diameter base

This Zakka-style drawstring pouch with a crocheted
base is the perfect size to carry essential items. It's also
an appropriate size to hold small crochet or knitting
projects for crafting on the go. It's decorated with
a coordinating fabric patch and leather label. Use this
opportunity to incorporate novelty-printed fabric from
your stash. What makes this pouch distinctive is the
combination of cotton, yarn and leather materials.

MATERIALS

1 skein of white cotton/acrylic 8-ply yarn

Fat quarter of lime novelty cotton
print for exterior bag

Fat quarter of polka-dot cotton
print for bag lining

Scrap of brown print, at least 4" × 15"
(10.2cm × 38.1cm), for casing

Scrap of brown gingham for label,
at least 3" × 3½" (7.6cm × 8.9cm)

Scrap of white felt, at least
2½" × 3" (6.4cm × 7.6cm)

Leather or fabric label

2 yards (1.8m) of white cord

2 small wooden beads

Brown embroidery thread

TOOLS & SUPPLIES

Basic sewing tools (see Tools and Materials)

Pinking shears

Crochet hook, size F (3.75 mm)

Note: All seam allowances are ¼" (6mm) unless indicated otherwise.

CUTTING AND PREPARING FABRICS

From the following, cut

- One 20½" × 9½" (52.1cm × 24.1cm) rectangle from the lime print fabric
- Two 12" × 2" (30.5cm × 5.1cm) strips from the brown print fabric
- One 3" × 3½" (7.6cm × 8.9cm) rectangle from the brown gingham

From the polka-dot print fabric, cut

- One 20½" × 9½" (52.1cm × 24.1cm) rectangle
- One circle 6¼" (15.9cm) in diameter

ABBREVIATIONS

sc: single crochet
dc: double crochet
sl st: slip stitch

CROCHET THE BASE OF THE BAG

1 Crochet an octagonal base using the pattern below.

Ch 5 and join into a ring with a sl st.

Row 1: Ch 2, work 15 dc into ring and join with a sl st.

Row 2: (Ch 2, 1 dc, ch 1, 2 dc) into first st, skip 1 st; *(2 dc, ch 1, 2 dc) into next st, skip 1 st, repeat from * 6 times, sl st to join.

Row 3: (Ch 2, 1 dc, ch 1, 2 dc) into first ch space; *1 dc into next space (between 4 dc group); (2 dc, ch 1, 2 dc) into next ch space, repeat from * 7 times, 1 dc into last space, sl st to join.

Row 4: (Ch 2, 1 dc, ch 1, 2 dc) into first ch space; 1 dc into next 2 dc spaces between 4 dc groups. (2 dc, ch 1, 2 dc) into next ch space, rep from * 7 times, 1 dc into next 2 dc spaces between last 4 dc group, sl st to join.

Row 5: (Ch 2, 1 dc, ch 1, 2 dc) into first ch space; 1 dc into next 3 dc spaces between 4 dc groups. (2 dc, ch 1, 2 dc) into next ch space, rep from * 7 times, 1 dc into next 3 dc spaces between last 4 dc group, sl st to join.

Row 6: (Ch 2, 1 dc, ch 1, 2 dc) into first ch space; 1 dc into next 4 dc spaces between 4 dc groups. (2 dc, ch 1, 2 dc) into next ch space, rep from * 7 times, 1 dc into next 4 dc spaces between last 4 dc group, sl st to join.

Row 7: Work 1 sc into each dc and ch. Fasten off.

2 Measure the diameter of the crocheted base at its widest point. It should measure approximately 6¼" (15.9cm). As the crocheted base has some stretch, a small variation will not affect the end product. If your base is too big, unravel a row of the crocheted base. If it is too small, add another row of crochet repeating the pattern.

3 Weave in the ends of the yarn.

ASSEMBLE THE EXTERIOR OF THE BAG

4 Position the leather label in the middle of the white felt scrap and hand-stitch in place using matching embroidery thread. Cut around the white felt using pinking shears. Position the felt in the middle of the gingham rectangle and machine-stitch in place using a small stitch length and a scant seam allowance. Press under the raw edges of the gingham rectangle. Position the label unit in the center of the green print fabric, approximately 2½" (6.4cm) above the bottom edge. Stitch in place to secure.

5 Serge or zigzag along the raw edges of the green print. Pin the short sides together with right sides facing. Stitch together using a ¼" (6mm) seam allowance so that you have a cylinder shape. Press open the seam allowance.

6 Fold the crocheted base into 4 quarters and mark each quarter with a pin so you have 4 equal quadrants. Create 4 even creases on the bottom edge of the exterior tube.

7 Turn the pouch exterior wrong-side out. Pin the crocheted base to the bottom of the exterior fabric with right sides facing and match the marks on the exterior with the quadrants of the base. Baste in place. It is important that the fabric is basted to row 7 of the crocheted base. Using your sewing machine, stitch the exterior fabric to the base, using a scant seam allowance (approximately ⅛" [3mm]). As the exterior fabric has been serged, only a narrow allowance is required. The crocheted base should stretch to fit the tube if required (Figure 1).

8 Fold under 1" (2.5cm) at each end of both the brown printed strips and press. Fold the strip in half lengthwise and press. These strips will become the channel that the drawstring is threaded through. Pin the folded channel strips to the top of the pouch with the raw edges aligned. The seam in the pouch is positioned in the middle of one of the strips. The end of one channel strip should be positioned near to the start of the other channel strip. Baste in place (Figure 2).

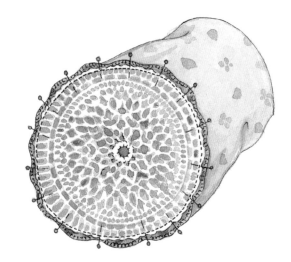

Figure 1

Figure 2

LABELS

Leather labels can be purchased from large sewing chain stores and from Etsy. Alternatively repurpose a label from a preloved item of clothing such as a pair of jeans.

ASSEMBLE THE LINING

9 Serge or zigzag along the raw edges of the lining. Pin the short sides of the lining rectangle together with right sides facing. Stitch them together using a ¼" (6mm) seam allowance so you have a cylinder shape, and leave a 4" (10.2cm) gap in the middle of the seam for turning. Press the seam allowance open.

10 Fold the circular base of the lining into 4 quarters and mark each quarter with a pin so you have 4 equal quadrants. Create 4 even creases on the bottom edge of the lining tube. Turn the lining wrong-side out. Pin the lining base to the bottom of the lining fabric, matching the creases on the bottom edge with the pins on the base. Stitch the lining fabric to the lining base using a ¼" (6mm) seam allowance. Press the lining.

11 Place the exterior of the pouch inside the pouch lining with right sides facing. The channel strips should be sandwiched in the middle of the exterior, and the lining fabrics should have their right sides together. Stitch along the top opening of the pouch using a ¼" (6mm) seam allowance. Turn the pouch right-side out through the opening in the lining. Using a whipstitch, close up the opening and press the lining.

MAKE THE DRAWSTRING

12 Cut the cord into 2 lengths, each measuring approximately 30" (76.2cm). Using a bodkin or a safety pin attached to one end of the cord, thread the cord through both channels. Thread a small bead onto both ends of the cord. Tie the ends together. Insert the other piece of cord into the opening on the opposite side and thread the cord through both channels. Thread a small bead onto the ends of the cord and tie the ends together.

ZAKKA

Zakka is a Japanese term that refers to a design style that encompasses everyday practical items or miscellaneous goods. Handmade zakka generally combines natural fibers and small embellishments. It's all about the details.

Cathedral Window Pincushions

DIFFICULTY
★ ★ ★

FINISHED SIZE
4" (10.2cm) square

These sweet pincushions feature the classic Cathedral Window block and incorporate small pieces of fine floral lawn. If you have ever wanted to learn Cathedral Window patchwork, this is a great project for learning the technique before embarking on a full-size pillow or quilt. The pincushions are fun to make and are perfect gifts for your crafty friends.

MATERIALS (makes 1 pincushion)

Fat quarter of white quilter's muslin

Scrap of floral lawn or quilting cotton, at least 6" (15.2cm) square

Scrap of white cotton batting, at least 2" (5.1cm) square

Polyester fiberfill or your stuffing of choice

TOOLS & SUPPLIES

Basic sewing tools (see Tools and Materials)

Chopstick

CATHEDRAL WINDOW PATCHWORK

Cathedral Window patchwork is a traditional quilt design that, historically, was made using feed sacks. The pattern fabric shows through the window frame and gives a stained glass window effect.

Note: All seam allowances are ¼" (6mm) unless otherwise noted.

CUTTING AND PREPARING FABRICS

From the following, cut

- Five 4½" (11.4cm) squares from white quilter's muslin for the cathedral window foundations
- Four 1" (2.5cm) squares from the batting for the cathedral windows

From the floral fabric, cut

- Four 1⅛" (2.9cm) squares for the cathedral windows
- One 4½" (11.4cm) square for the pincushion back

MAKE CATHEDRAL WINDOW FOUNDATION

1 To prepare the window foundations, fold a white 4½" (11.4cm) square in half, right sides together. Sew across both short ends. Refold the rectangle so the seams are in the center front and back, and sit on top of each other.

2 Stitch the raw edges, starting from the folded edge and working toward the center. Stop stitching ¾" (1.9cm) from the center on each side. Trim the points off each corner (Figure 1).

3 Turn the square right-side out through the opening using a turning tool or chopstick to poke out all the corners. Slipstitch the opening closed and press. Fold each corner into the center of the block and press. This is the front of the block (Figure 2).

4 Repeat steps 1–3 for 3 more squares.

5 Match 2 squares with their "backs" together. The sides with the folded corners should be facing out. Unfold one corner on each square and sew the squares together along the crease line. Backstitch at the beginning and end of each seam (Figure 3).

6 Repeat step 5 with another 2 squares so that you have 2 rows of 2 squares. Fold out the top points on the rows, as in Figure 3. Place two rows together with folds facing out and flat fabric together. Stitch across the base of the points as you did for the single pieces (Figure 4).

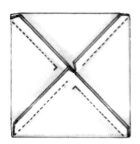

Figure 1

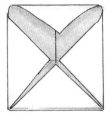

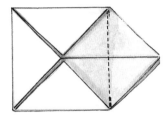

Figure 2   Figure 3

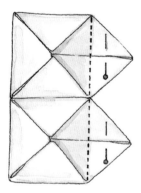

Figure 4

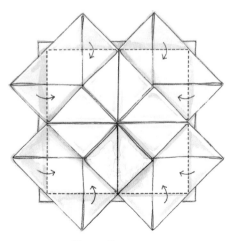

Figure 5

7 Center your panel of 4 cathedral window foundations onto the last remaining white square. You'll need a ¼" (6mm) border around the outside of the cathedral foundation panel. Unfold the flaps on the outer edge of the squares around the edge of the panel and use the same technique to sew that panel to the white fabric square (Figure 5).

8 After stitching the folded foundation to the base, fold the points back down and hand-stitch the 4 points together in the center of each of your 4 folded squares. Use white thread and stitch securely (Figure 6).

STITCH CATHEDRAL WINDOWS

9 The windows are made with the 1⅛" (2.9cm) squares of floral print fabric. Center the 1" (2.5cm) square of batting on one of the squares formed by folded flaps on adjacent squares. Center a floral print square over the batting and pin to secure (Figure 7).

10 To stitch a window, fold the edge of the 4 flaps surrounding the window patch over the raw edge of the window patch. In the center of each edge of the window patch, the fold should be ³⁄₁₆" (5mm) wide, tapering towards each corner. Blindstitch the edge in place, starting and ending ³⁄₁₆" (5mm) from each end (Figure 8). Repeat for all 4 windows.

ASSEMBLE PINCUSHION

11 Position the 4½" (11.4cm) floral square on a flat surface with the right side facing up. Place the Cathedral Window panel face down on the floral fabric with all the raw edges aligned and pin the sides together. Stitch around the outside of the square, leaving a 2" (5.1cm) gap in one side for turning. Clip the corners. Carefully turn the pincushion right-side out using a chopstick or turning tool to push out the corners. Press. Fill with stuffing and then slipstitch the opening in the pincushion closed.

Figure 6

Figure 7

Figure 8

CHAPTER 5

For Kids

I rediscovered sewing when my children were young. Nothing was more enjoyable than sewing toys and clothing for them. Handmade toys and baby items are so much nicer than the mass-produced goods available today. Your children will enjoy playing with *Ladybug Beanbags*, storing their treasures in the *Pretty Panda Snap Purse* or *Nautical Treasure Bags*, and wearing a playful *Boutique Baby Bib*. These projects make lovely gifts for the little people in your life.

Buttons and other small items may present choking hazards for children under three years of age. When making these projects for a young child, replace such supplies with child-safe options where you feel it's appropriate.

Ladybug Beanbag Game

DIFFICULTY

★ ☆ ☆

FINISHED SIZE

5" × 6" (12.7cm × 15.2cm)

These bright ladybug beanbags are great for preschool play and can be used to develop hand-eye coordination and motor skills. Toss them through a hoop, stack them, hide them—the possibilities for play are endless! Made from wool felt and coordinating fabric, they are filled with stuffing pellets.

MATERIALS (makes a set of 6 beanbags)

½ yard (45.7cm) of red wool felt for ladybug body

Fat quarter of black wool felt for ladybug head and spots

Assorted red and white cotton fabric scraps, measuring at least 4" (10.2cm) square

4 cups of stuffing pellets (or other stuffing material of your choice, such as dried beans, uncooked rice, etc.)

Black embroidery thread

TOOLS & SUPPLIES

Basic sewing tools (see Tools and Materials)

Cardboard

Spray starch

Embroidery needle

TEMPLATES

Ladybug Top, Bottom, Head, Spots, Tail, and Pressing Template (on CD)

Note: Seam allowances are 1/8" (3mm) wide unless otherwise indicated.

CUTTING AND PREPARING FABRICS

From fabrics, cut

- 6 circles from red felt using the Ladybug Bottom template
- 6 pieces from red felt using the Ladybug Top template
- 6 circles from black felt using the Ladybug Head template
- 36 circles from black felt using the Spots template
- 6 tails from the assorted red/white fabric scraps using the Tail template

Trace the Pressing Template onto cardboard and cut it out.

ASSEMBLE THE LADYBUGS

1 Moisten the curved edge of the fabric tail with spray starch. Position the tail with the wrong side facing up on the ironing board. Position the Pressing Template on top of the tail so the tip and sides are aligned. Press the fabric seam allowance of the tail over the curved edge of the card so the seam allowance is pressed flat and it retains its curved shape. Repeat for the remaining 5 fabric tails.

2 Pin the fabric tail to the underside of the ladybug top so that the printed fabric is facing up and the curved edge of the tail is aligned with the curved edge of the felt top to complete its circular shape (refer to the photograph for placement). Stitch the tail to the top piece of felt along both straight edges of the wedge. Repeat for the remaining ladybugs.

SO MUCH FUN!

Beanbags can be used in endless games to promote skill development in young children. They can be balanced on their heads, tossed through a hoop, used for throwing and catching practice, used in beanbag relay races and used in hide-and-seek. There's lots of fun to be had for little ones!

3 Pin 6 black spots to the top of the ladybug, as shown in the photograph. Use 2 strands of embroidery thread and a blanket stitch to stitch around each spot to secure it to the felt top. Repeat for the remaining ladybugs.

4 Position the top piece of the ladybug on top of the ladybug bottom so that the circles are aligned. Insert a black circle for the ladybug head in between the 2 layers so that half of the circle is covered by the red felt. Pin them to secure. Stitch around the outside of the ladybug using ⅛" (3mm) seam allowance, leaving a 2" (5.1cm) gap on one side. Repeat for the remaining ladybugs.

5 Fill the ladybug with ½ cup plus 1 tablespoon of stuffing pellets. Stitch the gap in the ladybug closed. Repeat for the remaining ladybugs.

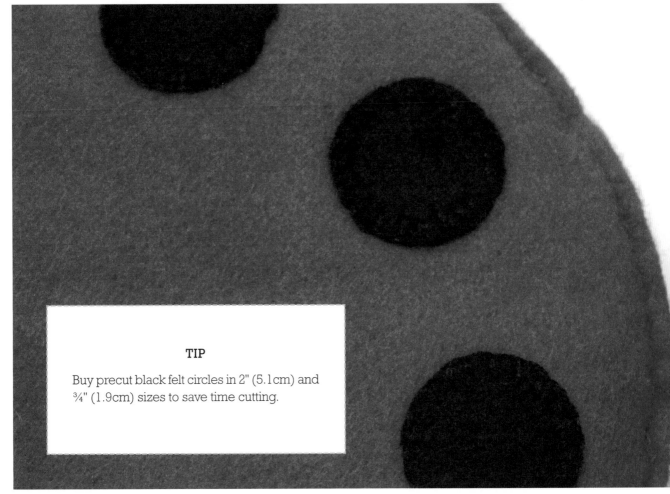

TIP

Buy precut black felt circles in 2" (5.1cm) and ¾" (1.9cm) sizes to save time cutting.

Pretty Panda Snap Purse

DIFFICULTY
★ ★ ☆

FINISHED SIZE
5½" × 4½" (14cm × 11.4cm), excluding ears

Pandas are universally popular. Children will love this cute pouch, which features a darling appliquéd panda and a handy snap closure.

MATERIALS (for 1 pouch)

Fat eighth of cotton fabric for pouch exterior

Fat eighth of white homespun for pouch lining

Fat eighth of fusible fleece

Scrap of gingham fabric, at least 6" × 4" (15.2cm × 10.2cm), for ears

Scrap of black fabric, at least 2½" × 4" (6.4cm × 10.2cm), for outer eyes

Scrap of white fabric, at least 1½" × 3" (3.8cm × 7.6cm), for inner eyes

Scrap of black fabric, at least 1½" × 1" (3.8cm × 2.5cm), for nose

Scrap of black fabric, at least 5" × 8" (12.7cm × 20.3cm), for the casing

2 black sequins

Black embroidery thread

4½" × ½" (11.4cm × 1.3cm) flex frame

TOOLS & SUPPLIES

Basic sewing tools (see Tools and Materials)

Cardboard

Spray starch

Embroidery needle

Long-nose pliers

TEMPLATES

Pouch, Outer Eyes, Inner Eyes, Nose, and Ears (on CD)

Note: Seam allowances are ¼" (6mm) wide unless otherwise indicated.

CUTTING AND PREPARING FABRICS

Using the Pouch template, cut

- 2 pieces from the white printed fabric for the pouch exterior
- 2 pieces from the white homespun for the pouch lining
- 2 pieces from the fusible fleece

From the black print fabric, cut four 5" × 2" (12.7cm × 5.1cm) strips for the casing.

Using the Ear template, cut 4 pieces from the black gingham.

Trace the Inner Eye, Outer Eye, and Nose shapes onto cardboard and cut them out. These cardboard shapes will be used to appliqué the facial features.

Using the Outer Eye cardboard shape as a template, cut out 2 outer eyes from black print fabric. Add a ¼" (6mm) seam allowance around the outside of the template.

Using the Inner Eye cardboard shape as a template, cut out 2 inner eyes from white print fabric. Add a ¼" (6mm) seam allowance around the outside of the template.

Using the Nose shape cardboard as a template, cut out 1 nose from black print fabric. Add a ¼" (6mm) seam allowance around the outside of the template.

APPLIQUÉ POUCH

1 Fuse the fleece onto the back of the exterior pouch pieces, ensuring all edges are aligned.

2 Position the Outer Eye cardboard template onto the back of the corresponding fabric piece so it's centered. Moisten the edges of the fabric with spray starch. Using your iron, press the seam allowance of the eye over the cardboard. Work your way around the outside of the eye with the iron, pressing the seam allowance over the cardboard so it's flat. Repeat for the remaining outer eye.

3 Using the same technique as described in step 2, prepare the inner eye pieces and the nose.

4 Referring to the photograph of the pouch for placement, position the nose and eye pieces on the pouch exterior and pin to secure. Hand-stitch the outer eyes, inner eyes and nose in position. Stitch a sequin to both inner eyes, as shown in the photograph. Using black embroidery thread, stitch the mouth in place below the nose, using an outline stitch.

5 Pin 2 ear pieces together with the right sides facing. Stitch around the outside of the ear. Clip curves and turn the ear right-side out. Press the ear. Repeat to construct the other ear. Using the photograph of the panda, position the ears on each side approximately ½" (1.3cm) down from the top edge so the raw edges are aligned and the ears are folded over the eyes (Figure 1).

Figure 1

ASSEMBLE THE POUCH

6 Pin the front and back of the pouch together with the right sides facing and all the edges aligned. Stitch the sides and bottom of the pouch together, leaving the top edge open. Clip the curves, turn the pouch right-side out and press. Pin both pieces of the lining together and stitch them in the same manner, leaving a 4" (10.2cm) gap at the bottom of the pouch for turning. Clip the curves and press.

7 To make the casing for the pouch, place 2 of the rectangles together with right sides facing. Pin and stitch along the short edges. Turn the piece right-side out and press. Fold the rectangle in half lengthwise and press. Repeat with the 2 remaining casing rectangles.

8 Pin one of the casing strips to the top edge of the pouch front so that it's centered and the raw edges are aligned. Baste in place with an ⅛" (3mm) seam allowance. Baste the remaining casing strip to the back of the pouch in the same way.

9 Place the exterior of the pouch inside the lining so the right sides are facing. Pin the lining to the pouch exterior around the top opening. Stitch around the opening. Turn the pouch right-side out through the gap in the lining. Stitch the gap in the lining closed using a slipstitch. Press.

10 Carefully slide one prong of the snap frame through one casing, and the other prong through the remaining casing. Following manufacturer's instructions, insert the pin in place at the open end of the frame to secure. You will need long-nose pliers to close the snap frame.

TIP

You can purchase purse flex frames (also known as purse snap frames) from Etsy or check with your local fabric shop.

Nautical Treasure Bags

DIFFICULTY
★★☆

FINISHED SIZE
8½" × 7½" (21.6cm × 19cm)

Children will delight in storing their treasures in these nautical-inspired drawstring bags. Featuring a simple sailboat appliqué and rickrack trim, they are perfectly sized to use as a party favor bag. The base of the bag was inspired by a coffee bag with a stand-up bottom.

MATERIALS (makes 1 bag)

Fat eighth of quilting cotton for the base of the bag (Fabric A)

Fat eighth of quilting cotton for the top of the bag and the appliqué foundation (Fabric B)

4 scraps of cotton prints in red, blue, navy and gray, measuring at least 3½" (8.9cm) for appliqués

⅔ yard (61cm) of white cotton cord

½ yard (45.7cm) of rickrack trim

Scrap of ½" (1.3cm) wide ribbon

Double-sided fusible web for appliqué

TOOLS & SUPPLIES

Basic sewing tools (see Tools and Materials)

Appliqué mat (optional)

Iron and ironing board

TEMPLATES

Sailboat Appliqué (on CD)

Note: Seam allowances are ¼" (6mm) wide unless otherwise indicated.

CUTTING & PREPARING FABRICS

- Using Fabric A, cut one 9" × 8½" (22.9cm × 21.6cm) rectangle for the base of the bag
- Using Fabric B, cut two 7" × 8½" (17.8cm × 21.6cm) rectangles for the appliqué foundation and the top of the bag
- Cut one 2" (5.1cm) length of ribbon
- Cut two 8½" (21.6cm) lengths of rickrack trim

APPLIQUÉ SAILBOAT

1 Using the appliqué template, trace the sailboat in reverse onto the paper side of the fusible web. Cut around the 4 shapes that form the sailboat, leaving a ¼" (6mm) clearance. Press them onto the back of 4 cotton scraps. Cut around the sailboat components.

2 Peel off the backing paper and position the sailboat appliqué onto one of the 7" × 8½" (17.8cm × 21.6cm) rectangles so that the sailboat is centered and located 1" (2.5m) above the bottom edge of the rectangle. Fuse the sailboat in place.

3 Stitch around the outside of the sailboat components using black thread. Stitch around each shape 3 times to create an outline and to secure the pieces.

ASSEMBLE BAG

4 Position the base of the bag on top of the appliqué, with the right sides facing and the bottom edges aligned. Pin to secure and then stitch the 2 pieces together. Serge (overlock) or zigzag to finish the edge. Stitch the other 7" × 8½" (17.8cm × 21.6cm) rectangle to the other side of the fabric base. Press both seams towards the base. Pin a length of rickrack along each seam and stitch it to secure.

5 Fold the piece of ribbon in half lengthwise and pin it on the top left-hand side so it's located 4" above the rickrack. Baste in place. Serge or zigzag around the outside of the bag to finish the raw edges (Figure 1).

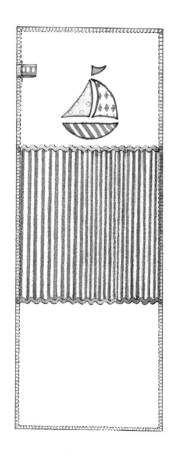

Figure 1

6 Fold the bag in half with the right sides facing. The rear of the appliqué will be facing up. Mark 1" (2.5cm) above the fold line. Fold the bottom of the bag up 1" (2.5cm) and press (Figure 2).

7 Stitch the right-hand side of the bag from the top to the bottom, catching the fold in the bottom of the pouch. On the left-hand side, stitch from ⅜" (1cm) above the ribbon tag to the bottom of the pouch.

8 Stitch the seam allowance in place around the opening at the top of the left seam (Figure 3).

9 Fold over ¼" (6mm) around the top opening of the bag and press. Fold over another ⅝" (1.6cm) around the top opening and press. Stitch around the top opening close to the fabric fold to secure the hem and create a channel for the drawstring. Thread the cord through the channel at the top of the pouch. Tie the ends of the cord in a knot.

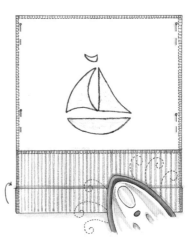

Figure 2

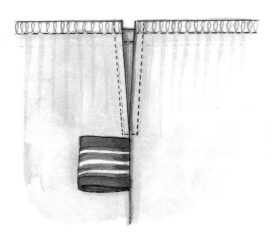

Figure 3

TIP

Try customizing a baby bib with the sailboat appliqué.

Boutique Baby Bibs

DIFFICULTY
★ ★ ☆

FINISHED SIZE
10" × 12½" (25.4cm × 31.8cm)

These delightful baby bibs feature a cute hexagon flower and simple stitching. Made from quilting cotton, they contain a layer of absorbent flannel in the lining and include a snap fastener for quick release. These boutique-style baby bibs make a lovely and useful baby shower gift.

MATERIALS (for 1 bib)

2 fat eighths of quilting cotton for bib front

1 fat quarter of quilting cotton for bib back

9 scraps of quilting cotton, measuring at least 3" × 4" (7.6cm × 10.2cm) for hexies and tab

1 fat quarter of plain white flannel for lining

1 package of bias binding (or make your own from a fat quarter of quilting fabric)

1 snap fastener set

Embroidery floss

TOOLS

Basic sewing tools (see Tools and Materials)

Paper hexagons (¾" [1.9cm] sides) or make your own from the template provided

Embroidery needle

TEMPLATES

Bib Front, Tab, Hexagon (on CD)

Note: Seam allowances are ¼" (6mm) wide unless otherwise indicated.

CUTTING AND PREPARING FABRICS

- Using the Bib Front template provided, cut 1 bib shape from the flannel.
- Flip the Bib Front template so the reverse side is facing up and use it to cut the lining.
- Cut the Bib Front template along the line as marked to form 2 parts for the bib front.
- Pin the top part of the Bib Front template to the bib front fabric. Cut it out, adding a ¼" (6mm) seam allowance along the bottom edge (where the template was cut).
- Pin the bottom part of the Bib Front template to fabric. Add a ¼" (6mm) seam allowance along the top edge (where the template was cut) and cut it out.
- Using the scrap fabrics, cut 7 hexagons using the larger Hexagon template.
- Using the Tab template, cut 2 tabs from fabric scraps and 1 tab from the flannel fabric.

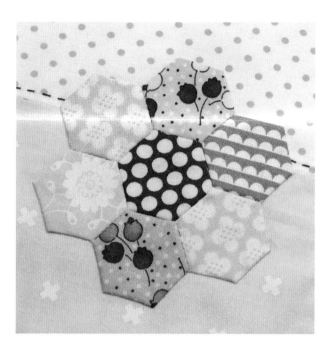

PREPARE HEXAGONS

1 Following the directions given in English Paper Piecing in the Techniques section, and using 7 hexagon papers with ¾" (1.9cm) sides, prepare 7 small hexagons. Stitch the hexagons together using a whipstitch so that they form a flower shape. Press them and carefully remove the papers.

ASSEMBLE THE BIB

2 Place the 2 pieces that will form the bib front together with right sides facing and the straight edge aligned. Pin them together and stitch. Press the seam open. Take a fabric tab piece and position it at the top opening with right sides together and the straight edge aligned. Pin the tab in position and stitch the pieces together. Press with the seam open.

3 Using a water-soluble fabric pen, draw a straight line that is ⅛" (3mm) above the seam line on the bib front. Using 2 strands of embroidery thread and a running stitch, stitch along the line.

4 Refer to the template for placement of the hexagon flower. Place the hexagon flower in position on the front of the bib, and hand-stitch it in place using a whipstitch. Press (Figure 1).

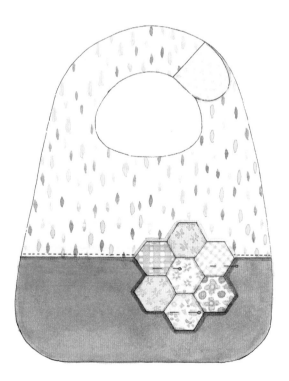

Figure 1

5 Stitch the tab to the backing piece as you did in step 2. Stitch the flannel tab to the flannel lining.

6 Position the backing face down on a flat surface. Place the flannel lining on top, aligning all raw edges, then place the bib front on top. Pin the layers together and baste around the outside using a scant seam allowance.

7 Unfold the bias binding and pin it around the outside of the bib front with the right sides facing. Stitch the bias binding to the bib front. Fold the bias binding over the back and pin it in place. Hand-stitch the back of the bias binding to the back of the bib.

8 Using an awl, make a small hole where you marked the placement of the snap. Position the snap components and secure them using a snap-setting tool.

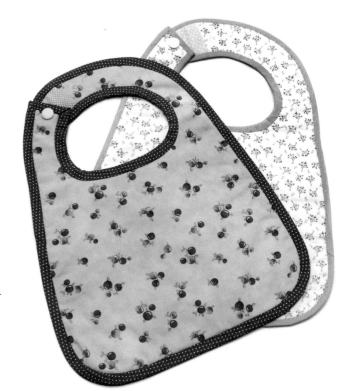

TIP

If you don't like installing snaps, use a button or Velcro closure.

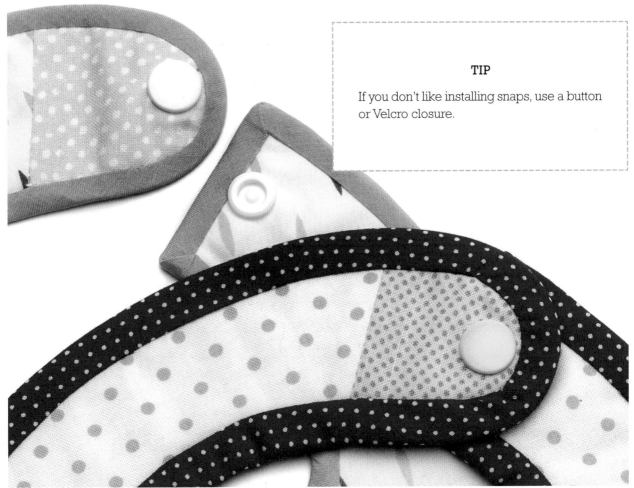

INDEX

RESOURCES

If you're looking for fabrics, materials and tools to make these projects, check out your local fabric, quilt and craft stores. Online shops, including Etsy, are also great resources. Don't forget to check out vintage markets, garage sales and thrift shops for some retro and vintage haberdashery supplies to add originality to your project. Or, if you're like me, consider collecting fabrics and supplies while traveling.

FABRICS

Dear Stella
www.dearstelladesign.com

Lecien Fabrics
www.lecien.co.jp/en/hobby

Liberty Fabrics
www.liberty.co.uk

Riley Blake Fabrics
www.rileyblakedesigns.com

Umbrella Prints
umbrellaprints.com.au/

Yuwa Fabrics
yuwafabrics.e-biss.jp

TOOLS AND SUPPLIES

Aurifil Threads
www.aurifil.com

Clover Notions
www.clover-mfg.com

DMC Embroidery Thread and Perle Cotton
www.dmc.com

Olfa Rotary Cutters and Mats
www.olfa.com

Olympus Sashiko Thread and Supplies
www.olympus-thread.com/original/English_site_map

Pellon Fusible Fleece (Wadding) and Interfacing
www.pellonprojects.com

Warm Company Batting and Insul-Brite
www.warmcompany.com

ACKNOWLEDGMENTS

It has always been a dream of mine to write a craft book. I am grateful for the opportunity to share my designs with like-minded sewists. I would like to thank the lovely people who read my blog, *A Spoonful of Sugar*, for their support and encouragement. From humble beginnings, *A Spoonful of Sugar* has grown and provided me with so many wonderful opportunities.

Thank you to all at F+W for your assistance in helping make this book a reality. Special thanks to my lovely editor, Noel Rivera, for all your help in creating the book; acquisitions editor, Amelia Johanson, for offering me the opportunity; Angela Atherton, for the gorgeous illustrations; Michelle Thompson for the stylish design; and Al Parrish and Joan Moyers for the beautiful photography and styling.

Special thanks to my wonderful mum, Maureen, and special nan, Kath, for teaching me everything I know about sewing, crochet, embroidery and craft work, and for getting me started on my craft journey.

I would like to thank my wonderful family—David, Brenton and Sarah—for your encouragement and enthusiasm. I couldn't have done it without you!

www.fwcommunity.com

a content + ecommerce company

20 19 18 17 16   5 4 3 2 1

Distributed in Canada by Fraser Direct
100 Armstrong Avenue
Georgetown, ON, Canada L7G 5S4
Tel: (905) 877-4411

Distributed in the U.K. and Europe by F&W MEDIA INTERNATIONAL
Brunel House, Newton Abbot, Devon, TQ12 4PU, England
Tel: (+44) 1626 323200
Fax: (+44) 1626 323319
Email: enquiries@fwmedia.com

Distributed in Australia by Capricorn Link
P.O. Box 704, S. Windsor NSW, 2756 Australia
Tel: (02) 4560 1600
Fax: (02) 4577 5288
E-mail: books@capricornlink.com.au

SRN: T5822
ISBN-13: 978-1-4402-4365-3

Edited by Noel Rivera
Designed by Michelle Thompson
Production coordinated by Jennifer Bass
Photography by Al Parrish
Photography styling by Joan Moyers
Illustrations by Angela Atherton

We make every effort to ensure the accuracy of our instructions, but errors occasionally occur. Errata can be found at www.sewingdaily.com/errata.

ABOUT THE AUTHOR

Since childhood, Lisa Cox has loved creating with fabric, yarn and thread. She works by day as an occupational therapist and is an avid crafter at night. Lisa shares her sewing, craft and baking projects on *A Spoonful of Sugar*, a blog she established with her daughter in 2008. Her sewing projects have been featured in a number of books, including *Just For You*, *Fabric-by-Fabric One-Yard Wonders*, *Pretty Little Presents* and *Sweet Nothings*. She has contributed to Better Homes and Gardens *Holiday Crafts* and is a regular contributor to *Stitch* and *Australian Homespun*. Lisa lives in Perth, Australia, with her husband and two children. Visit Lisa online at www.aspoonfulofsugardesigns.com.

METRIC CONVERSION CHART

To convert	to	multiply by
Inches	Centimeters	2.54
Centimeters	Inches	0.4
Feet	Centimeters	30.5
Centimeters	Feet	0.03
Yards	Meters	0.9
Meters	Yards	1.1

CHECK OUT OUR OTHER FANTASTIC SEWING TITLES!

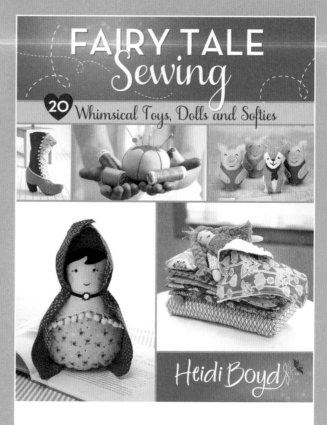

The Sewtionary
by Tasia St. Germaine
ISBN: 978-1-4402-3832-1
Price $29.99

Tasia St. Germaine of Sewaholic shares 101 of the most essential sewing terms and techniques. Presented in an easy-to-use format, this alphabetical reference gives more than just definitions; photographed step-by-step tutorials will guide you through each technique, showing you in detail how to apply the technique to your own projects. No matter what stage you're in on your sewing journey, *The Sewtionary* is here to help.

Fairy Tale Sewing
by Heidi Boyd
ISBN: 978-1-4402-3962-5
$24.99

Bring story time to life with this collection of imaginative projects. Drawing inspiration from classic fairy tales, author Heidi Boyd adds a modern twist to everything from huggable softies, such as the magical Unicorn, to interactive toys, such as Snow White's Cottage Tote. Sleeping Beauty's Castle Quilt brings sweet dreams to any child's room, and the Rapunzel Pillow is perfect for cuddling and play. Readily available cottons, felts, yarns and embroidery floss, plus clear instructions and detailed illustrations, make sewing simple and straightforward so you can spend less time sewing and more time enjoying your favorite fairy tales.

For more great books, magazines and projects, visit www.shopfonsandporter.com